403 BC

Ρ Σ Τ Υ Φ Χ Ψ Ω

ρ ασ τ υ φ χ ψ ω

r   s   t   u,y   f   ch   ps   ō

the script of the New Testament

Writing the Greek letters with pen and ink caused their shapes to change, so that styles called Greek Uncial, Greek Minuscule or lower-case, and Greek Cursive developed.

In early Christian times other alphabets were created from the Greek Uncial for translating the Bible into other languages.
    Coptic (Egyptian)
    Visigoth (Germanic - Ulfilas')
    Cyrillic (Slavic)
The Armenian and Georgian alphabets were also influenced by the Greek Uncial.

GREEK UNCIAL ALPHABET of 3rd to 9th cen. A.D. and 3 others derived from it

Greek Uncial	Phonetic Value	Coptic (Egyptian)	Visigoth (Germanic)	Early Cyrillic (Slavic)
		3rd Century A.D.	4th Century A.D.	9th Century A.D.

LETTERS DERIVED FROM OTHER SOURCES

*Demotic: a style of letters developed in Egypt through writing hieroglyphics rapidly with pen and ink on papyrus paper.
+Runic: an early Germanic alphabet of limited use.

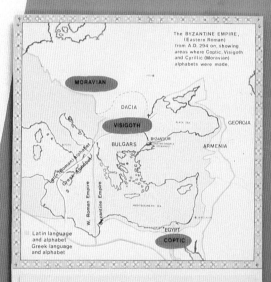

The BYZANTINE EMPIRE, (Eastern Roman) from A.D. 294 on, showing areas where Coptic, Visigoth and Cyrillic (Moravian) alphabets were made.

MORAVIAN
DACIA
VISIGOTH
BULGARS
GEORGIA
ARMENIA
EGYPT
COPTIC

Latin language and alphabet
Greek language and alphabet

The unmanageably large Roman Empire was divided in half by Diocletian in A.D. 282 for better administration. The division became permanent in A.D. 395.

This division meant that when the Western Empire fell in A.D. 476, it did not weaken the Eastern Empire, which kept on for another 1,000 years.

	WESTERN ROMAN EMPIRE	EASTERN ROMAN (BYZANTINE) EMPIRE
Capital	Rome	Byzantium/Constantinople/Istanbul
Church	Roman Catholic	Greek Orthodox
Language	Latin	Greek
Alphabet	Latin (Roman)	Greek

Shown here: a typical wall display from the Museum of the Alphabet, at the JAARS center in Waxhaw, North Carolina.

On the cover: Bishop Sahag confers with Mesrop Mashtotz on the translation of the Bible into Armenian, in the fifth century A.D. The first step was Mashtotz's development of the alphabet. Sculpture by Alan Baughman.

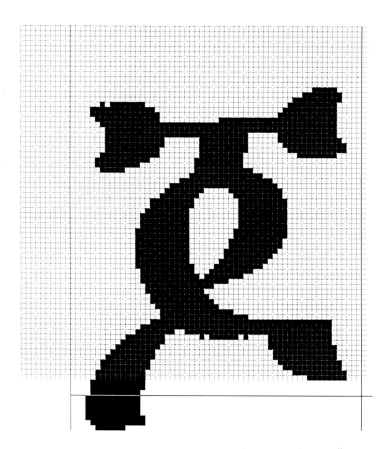

A computer adaptation of the letter ǰō, from the Ethiopic alphabet. (*See page 49 and 90.*)

A Presentation from
the Museum of the Alphabet
Waxhaw, North Carolina

The Alphabet Makers

Book Production Staff

Editor/Designer	Hyatt Moore
Photographer	Sonny Rains
Photographic Assistants	Dave Crough Bill Lambright
Writers	Katherine Voigtlander Karen Lewis
Editorial Assistants	Deborah Crough Betty Eastman Patricia Purvis Rich Kern Jane Pappenhagen Grace Watkins
Art Assistant	Barbara Alvarez
Special Assistance	Don Ziemer

For names of individuals responsible for the creation of the Museum of the Alphabet itself, see page 91.

Copyright 1990, 1991
First Edition, 1990
Second Edition, 1991
Library of Congress Catalog Number
90-71466

Summer Institute of Linguistics
P.O. Box 2727
Huntington Beach, California
92647, U.S.A.

ISBN 0-938978-13-6

Printed in the U.S.A.
Typography: Mediaeval Roman
by Redi-Type, Inc., Garland, Texas

Foreword

After many years on Pitcairn Island the last surviving member of the famous ship *Bounty* was discovered, along with a Fijian wife, a number of widows, and many children. As the story goes, Alexander Smith related to his first chronicler how he had been teaching the children many things, including how to read.

"I'll not forget," he said, "*how proud they was when they got so as they could read a few lines and write little messages to one another. Their mothers thought it was the wonder of the world, and when ye come to look at it, there's few things to equal the wonder of writin'. I'm blessed if I can see how men ever came to the knowledge of it in the first place.*"

That was over a century ago. But how many of us today, if we took the time Smith had to think about it, would come up with the same conclusion? The tools of reading and writing are a wonder. We tend to take them for granted and, like walking and talking, we don't remember learning any of them, though we use them continually.

The basis of literacy is some sort of writing system—usually an alphabet. Yet, for as long as they have been around, alphabets did not come with the original creation. They were conceived and invented by man. People with creative minds, bent on finding methods for better communication, worked them out for the good of all. Are these activities not imitations of the original Creator?

The book you hold, which you can read because of an alphabet, is about the amazing development of these systems. Specifically it is about their creators. It does not pretend to be exhaustive, and in some areas it cannot be much more than speculative. But it does give a taste of what has gone before us.

Though brief, the book is overfull. In that, it is like the museum it was designed to represent. In these 96 pages, and in the museum's 4900 square feet, virtually every alphabet strain is mentioned. The book and the museum span both time and cultures. They illustrate how writing systems need to be uniquely fitted to each language, and how these have been originally derived or adapted from others. In the end they also remind us that the process is not over. There are still many languages that do not have an alphabet at all. And without one, people with much to say, and often with great desire to learn from others, have no vehicle for literature. They are barred from the greater understanding and opportunities that literacy can bring.

It is to meet this challenge, and to serve the people who speak these languages, that Wycliffe Bible Translators and the Summer Institute of Linguistics exist. Following in a long history of alphabet makers, these modern linguists have developed alphabets in over 1000 languages in the last 50 years. They don't stop there, to be sure, but even if they did, they would have already planted the seed for amazing potential. As Alexander Smith said, there are few things to equal the wonder of writing.

—Hyatt Moore

Why an Alphabet Museum?

Cameron Townsend was dreaming. World renowned statesman, linguist, and visionary: he had always been a dreamer. As a boy he dreamed of flying. As a young man he dreamed of creating alphabets and giving people God's Word in their own language.

Now Townsend was dreaming of building a museum of alphabets. He wanted to help the world come to a genuine appreciation of the gift of writing systems. Most people, he believed, never think about the tools for reading and writing. They have no concept of what life would be like without an alphabet. And they have no idea that thousands of language groups around the world still have no way to write and read their own spoken language.

Land was available in the piney woods of North Carolina, a short hop, he felt, from the international diplomatic community of Washington, D.C. They, too, could visit and gain an enthusiasm for creating new alphabets for minority languages. And the diplomats could see that the organizations he had founded—The Summer Institute of Linguistics, Wycliffe Bible Translators, and JAARS (formerly *Jungle Aviation and Radio Service*)—stand ready to serve their countries. With his own eightieth birthday approaching and his organizations nearly 50 years old, Townsend recalled how it all began.

"There probably are about 500 minority languages that have no written form," he told his young recruits in the early 1930s. He exhorted them to move out, create alphabets, study the grammar, and begin to translate the Bible.

Today it is believed that there are as many as 3000 groups without a written form of their spoken language. How could Townsend have been so far short? The fact is, he had made a good guess based on what he had observed personally in Latin America. But a thorough survey of the world's languages was not available then, and linguistic information was limited. The science of linguistics itself was still in its infancy.

Pioneering soon became a hallmark of the Summer Institute of Linguistics (SIL). Not only did its members live in remote places but they began to make significant discoveries about languages and writing systems. Kenneth Pike's early discoveries in tone languages, for example, have helped other linguists around the world. Pike has gone on to give scholarly leadership to SIL and has had a broad influence in the field of linguistics. He has been nominated for the Nobel Peace Prize a number of times.

When Cameron Townsend first envisioned the Alphabet Museum, the Summer Institute of Linguistics had made major contributions to the alphabet-less peoples of the world. As a historian, he also admired four important linguists: Mashtotz of Armenia, Panini of India, Sejong of Korea, and Sequoyah of North America. Townsend knew any research team would discover strong historical ties between alphabets and Bible translation. Indeed, that's what happened.

When the Jews returned from the Babylonian exile, they had become accustomed to the Aramaic speech and alphabet. Many no longer understood Hebrew. When Ezra the Scribe read the Hebrew scriptures to them, he translated them into Aramaic (Nehemiah 8:8). Ezra is credited with starting to write Hebrew with the Aramaic alphabet. This is the origin of the Square Hebrew alphabet (450 B.C.). It eventually was used for making copies of the Old Testament and is the script for modern Israel today.

Late in the fourth century, the Visigoths, a warlike tribe, lived along the Roman frontier west of the

The Museum of the Alphabet, Waxhaw, North Carolina.

Black Sea. Many had become Christians, and Ulfilas, their bishop, saw they needed the Bible in their own language. For this, though, he first had to make an alphabet for writing the language. The Visigoths migrated west and were the first to conquer Rome in A.D. 410. Their aim was not so much to destroy but to share in the benefits of civilization. The translation of the Bible gradually transformed troublemakers into peacemakers.

In North America, in the mid-1800s, James Evans created an alphabet for the Cree Indians in order to translate the Bible. He tried to use Roman letters but the Cree sounds were too different from English. Eventually, Evans invented his own symbols. Cree

Katherine Voigtlander

words tend to be long; to shorten the writing, he used only one letter for each syllable. The Cree writing system turned out to be so simple that it is said one person could teach another in half a day. It spread through several other tribal groups across Canada. And capable Cree assistants helped Evans translate the Bible.

"This kind of information, tied in with people, is what makes the Alphabet Museum so interesting," says Richard Pittman, museum director. "When Cameron Townsend first proposed the idea to me, I thought it sounded boring. All I could see was four walls covered in alphabets. That's where Katie Voigtlander's genius came in. She could visualize how to make it exciting."

Richard Pittman, senior statesman with SIL, and Katherine Voigtlander, a trained artist and linguist, were an ideal team to create a museum about the alphabet makers. "Mr. Townsend really didn't give us any guidelines," continues Pittman. "So I came up with two: focus on the alphabet makers and select the stories first, not the artifacts. I felt the museum should have faces of alphabet makers as much as possible in order to make it come alive. I did not want to collect a lot of artifacts first and then try to tell a story about them. I felt we should do our research, select the stories, and then decide on the displays."

Cameron Townsend first suggested a 1000-square-foot building for the museum, but the initial research on alphabet makers convinced the staff that a larger structure would be needed. Today a 4900-square-foot brick building nestles against tall pine trees in Waxhaw, North Carolina. Original plans were to open the museum in 1982. For seven years, spring promised the completion, but the staff kept uncovering more information that begged to be included. Besides, there were few long-term staff

members to help. Katie Voigtlander was the only full-time worker. Literally hundreds of people, many of them non-SIL volunteers, gave their time and talents to the project. (See page 91 for listing.)

"It has been a pleasure to work on the Alphabet Museum," Pittman states. "It's thrilling to see the impact of alphabets on whole societies, indeed civilizations. I know that language is part of God's eternal design and I believe alphabets are part of the pattern."

Kenneth Pike was once asked why he did not leave SIL to work full time on linguistics. He responded: "I would not be doing linguistics if it weren't for Bible translation."

Over the years, SIL personnel have worked in over 1000 languages. Today over 6000 members of the Summer Institute of Linguistics and Wycliffe Bible Translators are involved in furthering the massive task of alphabet making, literacy work, and translation.

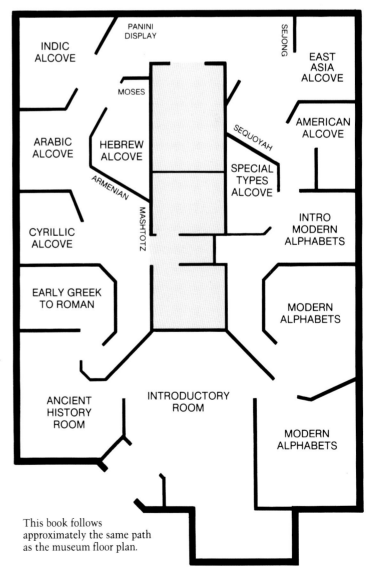

This book follows approximately the same path as the museum floor plan.

The Beginnings of Alphabets

Young Henry Rawlinson, dangling from ropes along the face of a cliff in Persia, copied a 60-foot cuneiform inscription King Darius had ordered chiseled there around 500 B.C. For the next 12 years, Rawlinson, a mid-nineteenth century British scholar, and others labored to crack the puzzle of cuneiform. At last they were able to read the linguistic conglomeration. The key to the first real writing system had been found.

About 50 centuries before Rawlinson's work, the ancient world began to see its first cities. As the complexities of urban living increased, frequent misunderstandings between merchants, traders, and religious leaders led to the need to write down information.

There are differing opinions as to why people felt the need to write. Some authorities think religion was the motivation. Others think that economics, the need to keep track of business transactions and inventories, was the reason for the beginnings of writing.

Early shipping records were kept on clay tablets. Cuneiform evolved from these beginnings in Mesopotamia as early as 3100 B.C. At first, impressions of tokens were pressed onto clay "envelopes." Later, symbols of the things to be itemized were scratched on flat clay tablets. Eventually, a squared-off stick was used to press wedge-shaped marks into the clay. Thus, the name cuneiform—from the Latin for "wedge."

About the same time, the Egyptian form of writing was developing. The Pharaohs must have enjoyed the "game" of reading. Reading hieroglyphics could be compared to several modern games combined: Some symbols were like *puns* in that they pictured a homonym (sun = son). Some were like a *rebus*, illustrating syllables (bee + leaf = belief). *Phonograms* used a picture for each letter of the word (cat + apple + rabbit + leaf = Carl). *Fish and fowl* used a picture to classify a word (cat = animal). Some pictures indicated a related idea (sun = daylight) as in the game of *Clue*. Others were to be taken literally (sun = sun), as in true picture reading.

Scholars tried to figure out this writing system after it had been "dead" for 1500 years. Finally, in 1822, Jean François Champollion, a French scholar, compared the Rosetta Stone and an obelisk inscription identifying the various reading games of the Egyptian hieroglyphics.

As time passed, these great early civilizations of the Bronze Age began to fade, and the eastern Mediterranean area then became the crossroads of the ancient Western world. The constant flow of merchandise, cultures, and writing systems demanded an easier way of writing. The first true alphabet was developed by Semitic people in this area between 1800 and 1300 B.C. For the first time, symbols representing single speech sounds constituted the whole of the writing system. This is the essence of an alphabet.

The original Sinaitic and Phoenician alphabets recorded only consonants as the Semitic languages did not need to write vowels. However, Greek could not be read with consonants alone, so the Greeks chose *some* Semitic consonants to represent their own consonants and used the extra symbols for vowels. The idea of writing vowels, which came from the Greeks, has had as much impact as anything else they gave us.

The Roman alphabet (which you are now reading) was developed by the Etruscans. They dominated the Italian peninsula before the Romans came into power, bridging the time from the Greeks to the Romans. Borrowing from the Greek alphabet, the Etruscans chose certain letter shapes and changed a few sound values for writing their own language.

The Romans, in turn, took over the Etruscan alphabet for writing Latin and passed it on to all Western European languages. Indeed, most of the peoples Rome conquered had unwritten languages. But with the spread of Christianity came the need to translate the Bible into other languages, and alphabets needed to be developed.

With the fall of Rome, Western Europe lapsed into illiteracy. Learning retreated to the monasteries, where monks spent endless hours hand-copying books. Writing became chaotic. One monk could not read what another had written, but copied it anyway.

Charlemagne was very concerned about

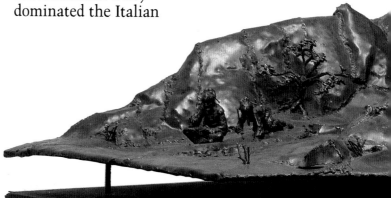

this trend. In 781 A.D. he invited Alcuin of York, an English scholar and churchman, to come and help. Alcuin's work in literacy probably did more to reverse the direction of the Dark Ages than any other event of his time.

Meanwhile, Eastern Europe began to seek its own alphabets. Mesrop Mashtotz tried desperately to fit other alphabets to his language, Armenian. Mashtotz wanted to strengthen Armenia, the first "Christian nation," against other religions and preserve ethnic unity. Finally, he "received the alphabet in a heavenly vision." Mashtotz and Bishop Sahag then translated the Bible and set up schools.

Prince Rostislav of the Slavic-speaking Moravians (central Czechoslovakia) sent a message to the Byzantine emperor in Constantinople: "We don't understand Latin or Greek. Please send us someone to teach us in our language."

The emperor sent two Greek brothers who knew Slavic. Two alphabets emerged. One fell into disuse, but the Cyrillic alphabet continues to be used widely. In the Soviet Union alone, more than 200 million people, representing more than 100 languages, use the Cyrillic alphabet.

And what of southwestern Asia? Aramaic, which had one of the earliest alphabets, became the common language of the vast area from Egypt to India as a result of the Assyrian and Persian conquests of the Arameans. As these

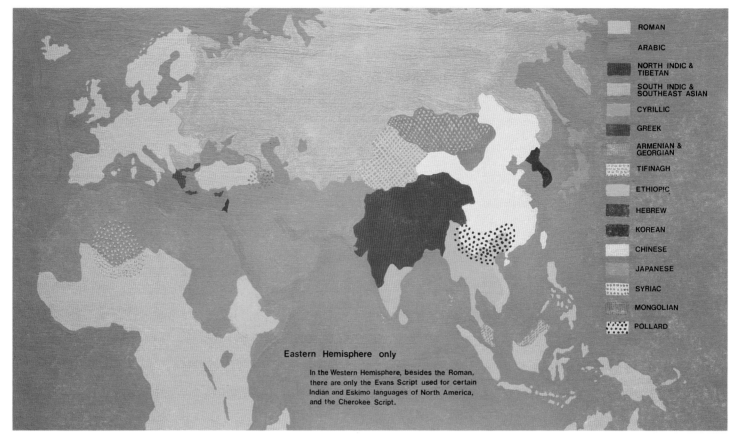

Eastern Hemisphere only

In the Western Hemisphere, besides the Roman, there are only the Evans Script used for certain Indian and Eskimo languages of North America, and the Cherokee Script.

Writing systems of the world today.

people were resettled by their conquerors, they took their alphabet with them. The Aramaic alphabet replaced other scripts and became the parent of most writing systems in the area, including Arabic.

The Arabic and Roman alphabets are cousins, descendants of their North Semitic grandfather. Like shorhand, Arabic is an efficient way of writing. All styles are cursive, geared to rapid penwork, and most vowels are not written. Certainly, Arabic is one of the most important alphabets in today's world, used by about 950 million people. After the Dark Ages, the European Renaissance resulted largely from the discovery of Europe's literary roots which were preserved in the Arabic alphabet and language at major Islamic centers.

Many scholars feel India's alphabets were also developed from the Aramaic alphabet—as a result of sea trade between Babylon and India (800-600 B.C.). The Brahmi alphabet makers analyzed their spoken language by charting the positions of the mouth as it moved in speech, noting location and manner of speech sound production. They assigned a letter to each sound.

Panini of India had a passion for listening to people around him and gathering illustrations of the use of language. Following in the steps of the Brahmi alphabet makers, he became the most renowned of grammarians. Though he lived sometime between the seventh and fourth centuries B.C., it was not until the discovery of his work by nineteenth-century Europe that linguistic science in the West was born. He is known as the "father of descriptive linguistics."

Africa is home to a third of all the world's languages. For over a thousand years, the Tuareg camel caravanners dominated the trade routes of the Sahara. They are descendants of the Numidians, who in the second century B.C. adopted the alphabet of their Phoenician conquerors, adding some of their traditional symbols as letters. They could write either right to left or bottom to top. Today the Tuareg people are adding vowels and reversing the direction of the original Tifinagh alphabet (see p. 50).

Africa has hundreds of tonal languages. In these, as in all the other tonal languages of the world, not only the consonants and vowels, but also the pitch of the voice distinguishes words.

Most of the original alphabets had letters to represent only consonants and vowels. Many tonal languages require tone to be written as well. This can be complicated.

For example, the Dan people of Côte d'Ivoire (Ivory Coast) had an intense desire to read their own language, but few could because the tones were not written.

Margrit Bolli, a linguist with the Summer Institute of Linguistics (SIL), struggled to find a solution for writing contour tones. Accent marks could not be used because both French, the national language, and Dan use them for vowel qualities. "How about numbers?" Bolli wondered. The people called it a "mathematical nightmare." The Dan considered the use of extra letters like *q, j,* and *x* a "language from Mars." Finally, everyone agreed on punctuation marks before and after syllables. A pleased reader said, "Those marks are like road signs to tell us which way to go." Now thousands read and write Dan, and the system is official for other languages as well.

E astern Asia also has writing systems uniquely designed to fit their special needs. The Korean alphabet is one of the most scientific ever created. King Sejong (A.D. 1397-1450), by naming his alphabet *Hun Min Jŏng Ŭm,* "Accurate Sounds (letters) to Educate the People," stated his purpose in making it. He invented new shapes for the letters, revealing in them profound linguistic insights. They were pictures of the parts of human anatomy that form speech—teeth, tongue, lips, cheeks, and throat. It is an excellent alphabet that represents the sounds of the spoken language and does so in an unusually systematic way.

Sejong wanted an easy way to write Korean so that all Koreans could be literate. However, other Korean men of learning opposed the alphabet because it was not like the Chinese they had traditionally used. Consequently, Sejong's alphabet was largely ignored until almost the twentieth century. Then the use of the alphabet for Bible translation helped popularize it. It is now official in both South and North Korea.

Emperor Fu-Hsi (2852-2738 B.C.) is the legendary inventor of the Chinese script. His was a pre-writing device made up of straight and broken lines said to be taken from the marks on a turtle shell. Chinese writing is the oldest system in the world today, having changed little in 4000 years. The characters are not symbols for individual sounds, as alphabet letters are, but for whole words, as if each word were pictured. It is a *logographic* or word-writing system.

Why would an alphabet not work for Chinese? First, the difference between Chinese dialects is as great as that between the French and Spanish languages. With an alphabet, Chinese would be written differently in each area. But the nonalphabetic writing system unites speakers of all Chinese dialects.

Second, Chinese is loaded with *homophones,* like the English *to, too,* and *two.* Most Chinese words sound like several, or even dozens, of other words. Since alphabets represent words by their sounds only, they have difficulty writing distinctively words that sound alike. But the Chinese system is ideally suited to handle homophones because the writing distinguishes both meaning and sound.

Third, an alphabet is ideal for writing languages that have small changeable parts of words, as in *write, unwritten, writer's,* and so forth. But Chinese words do not have changeable parts. Chinese grammar works by adding and rearranging words rather than by changing or adding parts of words. So the logographic system with unchanging symbols for whole words is fitting.

Modern Japanese is the most complex major writing system in use today. Its basis is the Chinese, which came via Korea in the fourth century A.D. *Kanji,* whole Chinese characters chosen for their meanings, are used in writing Japanese root words (nouns, adjectives, and verbs). *Kana,* abbreviated Chinese characters chosen for their sounds, are used in writing Japanese forms which cannot be written by *kanji.*

S equoyah, a North American Cherokee Indian (c. 1765-1843), though illiterate, created a writing system. Convinced that the white man's power lay in the written language, he determined to provide the same for his people.

How would one write his own language? By making a picture of each one of thousands of words? Sequoyah tried that. He drew symbols with pokeberry juice on chips of wood. But his wife, angered by his neglect of the family, threw the chips into a fire. Sequoyah decided to try a new method.

He noticed that just a few recurrent groups of sounds (syllables) combined to form numerous words. After 12 years of hard work, he completed a set of 85 symbols. Next he had to convince the tribal elders it would work. He taught his young daughter, Ahyoka, to read and write. Together they carried out a demonstration. Sequoyah left the house while Ah-yoka wrote

THE ALPHABET TREE

what the skeptical elders dictated. When Sequoyah returned and read what she had written the elders were dumbfounded, and then ecstatic. Their own language could be written!

Literacy caught on like wildfire among the Cherokee. Within months they were able to read and write in two languages (English and Cherokee), and a steady stream of literature poured from their own printing press.

The ancient writing systems of Mexico and Central America remain inadequately deciphered. However, their number systems and astronomical systems are well understood. The Mayans perfected a *calendar round*, a device that worked like three interlocking cogwheels of different sizes. Three cycles of 13, 20, and 365 days were correlated. The calendar was central

to Mayan planning for agriculture, religious rituals, and community affairs. It was more accurate than the Julian calendar of the Spaniards.

Many writing systems do not fall into the specific category of alphabets. The first written symbols of any kind were numbers devised to record inventories and business dealings. Number symbols, called numerals, are *ideographic*: one symbol per concept. Today's *place value* mathematical system originated in India. The number *zero* was invented to hold the place so that a number like 3030 was not confused with 33. The Arabs in Spain adopted the system in the ninth century A.D. and it spread throughout Europe. Without this invention, the industrial and scientific ages might not have been possible. The place value system is more widespread than the alphabet.

Other special writing systems include Braille for the blind and hand signing, the alphabet by which the deaf can "hear." The use of alphabet letters for writing music is another example of the many ways in which letters function. However, the earliest musical notation was written in cuneiform on a clay tablet circa 1400 B.C.

To decipher the alphabet of a dead language is noble; to design an alphabet for a living language is sublime," Richard Pittman said. Today over 300 million people still do not have a way to write their own language. They represent at least 2000 of the world's spoken languages. Linguists and other supporting personnel with the Summer Institute of Linguistics (SIL) are involved in hundreds of language projects developing alphabets, analyzing the grammar of these languages, translating literature and the scriptures, and encouraging literacy.

Many SIL linguists have encountered unusual situations in their language projects. Frank and Ethel Robbins discovered that the Quiotepec Chinantec people of Mexico do not necessarily have to open their mouths to speak. "Blowing" sounds through their noses communicates as clearly as the commonly spoken words. Also in Mexico, the Mazatecs have developed a "whistle talk." SIL linguists Eunice Pike and George and Florrie Cowan realized the importance of tone when they heard the Mazatecs carry on sustained conversations by whistling (see p. 79).

The ancient Cham alphabet in Vietnam may be the earliest on the southeastern Asia mainland. The Cham, desiring to preserve their heritage, asked SIL linguists David and Doris Blood to produce literature in their alphabet. They place high value on their language, alphabet, and literature as a tie to their past splendor.

The curiosity that drove Henry Rawlinson to dangle from ropes, the power the Cherokee Indians felt as they read and wrote their own language, the pride the Cham have in their heritage, and the magic of making an intangible spoken language tangible by writing it down are what motivate people all over the world to learn to read and write.

There is no end to the surprises the alphabet will bring if mixed with discretion and read with wondering.

—H. M. Tomlinson

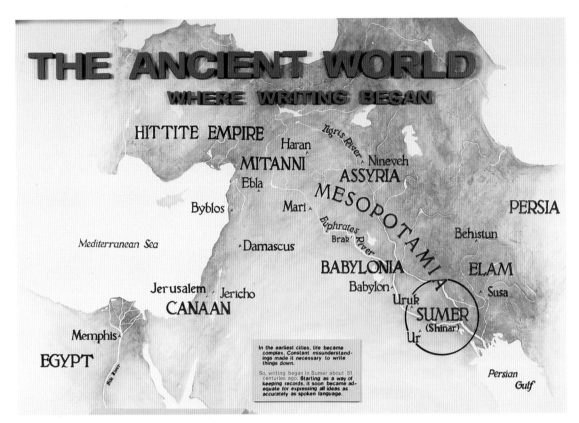

THE ANCIENT WORLD
WHERE WRITING BEGAN

HITTITE EMPIRE

Haran

Tigris River

MITANNI

Ebla

Nineveh

ASSYRIA

MESOPOTAMIA

Byblos

Mari

PERSIA

Mediterranean Sea

Euphrates River

Brak

Behistun

Damascus

BABYLONIA

ELAM

Jerusalem

Jericho

Babylon

Susa

CANAAN

Uruk

SUMER
(Shinar)

Memphis

Ur

EGYPT

Nile River

Persian Gulf

In the earliest cities, life became complex. Constant misunderstandings made it necessary to write things down.

So, writing began in Sumer about 51 centuries ago. **Starting as a way of keeping records, it soon became adequate for expressing all ideas as accurately as spoken language.**

(*Above*) A clay tablet written in Sumerian cuneiform about 2150 B.C. It contains the world's oldest medical prescriptions, 15 in all. Some are poultices, some plant and beer mixtures to drink.

ROOTS OF CUNEIFORM

Clay tokens representing goods being shipped . . .

Scratched on clay with a pointed stick

. . . were sealed in clay "envelopes," with their impressions on the surface.

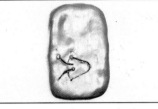

. . . symbols were later turned sideways.

Later, flattened clay was used as "writing tablets."

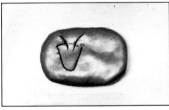

Still later, marks were pressed in with a squared-off stick, making the abstract shapes of cuneiform.

This cuneiform inscription of 2065 B.C. reads: "(For the) god Sullat and (for the) god Hanish, his lord, did Shulgi, mighty man, King of Ur, King of Sumer and Akkad, build this temple."

(*Below*) A reconstruction of the ruins of a library in Nineveh discovered by A.H. Layard in 1849.

MESOPOTAMIAN CUNEIFORM

3100 B.C.

Cuneiform was a combination writing system composed of *pictograms* and *ideograms* (idea symbols) and *phonograms* (sound symbols). The cuneiform system began as pictures and continued, in part, to convey meaning the way pictures do.

This symbol for *king* is:

Originally a picture of a king, it had the same form but was said differently in many different languages: *Lugal* in Sumerian, *Šarru* in Assyrian and Babylonian, *Haššu* in Hittite.

Because of the need to write names unambiguously, the phonographic system, or writing by speech sounds, forced its way into cuneiform. For this words were written, As words were written, only their sounds were considered, not their meanings.

The symbols and meaning of Hammurabi's name are:

ha + am + mu + ra + bi
('fish' + 'wild bull' + 'year' + '?' + 'innkeeper')

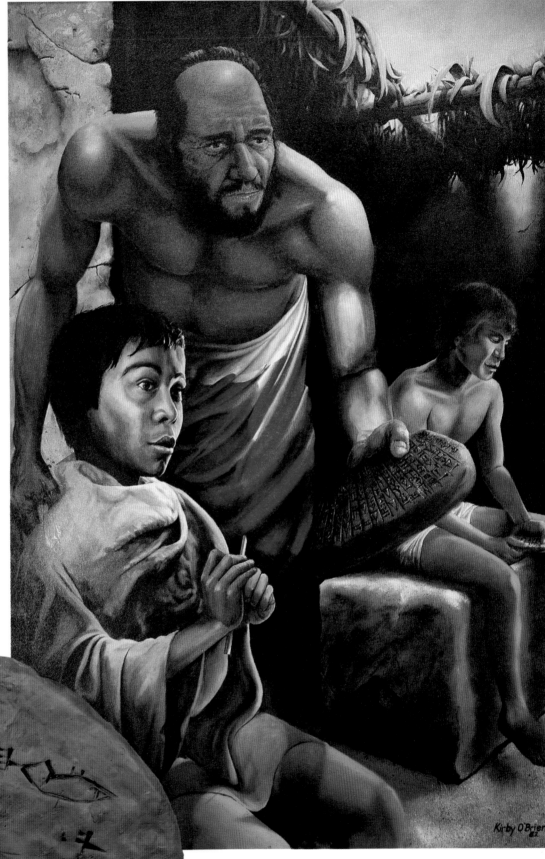

(*Left*) A Sumerian schoolboy's attempt, about 2600 B.C. Compare the writing of *king* with an accurate rendition (*above left*). The pictographic *king* can be recognized by the crown.

(*Above*) A Sumerian school, the earliest on earth, called an *edubba* (tablethouse). Here boys studied 12 years to become scribes in the cuneiform script.

Hope has long been abandoned of deciphering hieroglyphs.
—David Akerblad, 1802

Je tiens l'affaire. ("I've got it.")
—Jean Francois Champollion, 1822

EGYPTIAN HIEROGLYPHICS
PICTURE WRITING
3000 B.C.

S cholars tried to figure out this writing system after it had been "dead" for 1500 years. The symbols were such realistic pictures that for years they were thought to symbolize what they looked like. But the symbols could not usually be read as the things they pictured.

In *form* the system had not evolved beyond pictures, but in *function* it had evolved into a combination system like cuneiform.

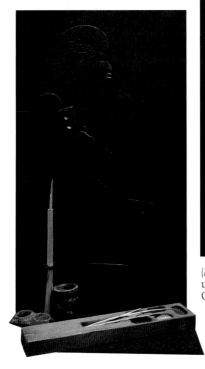

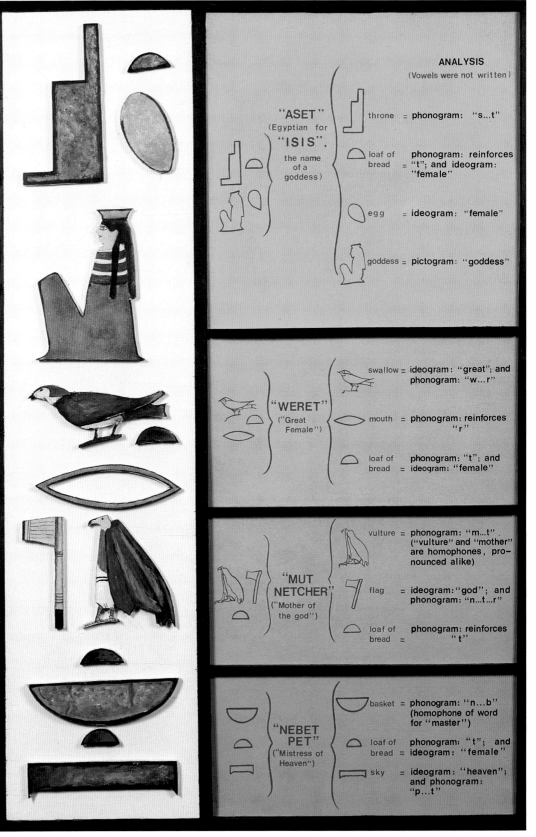

ANALYSIS
(Vowels were not written)

"ASET" (Egyptian for **"ISIS"**, the name of a goddess)

throne	= phonogram: "s...t"
loaf of bread	= phonogram: reinforces "t"; and ideogram: "female"
egg	= ideogram: "female"
goddess	= pictogram: "goddess"

"WERET" ("Great Female")

swallow	= ideogram: "great"; and phonogram: "w...r"
mouth	= phonogram: reinforces "r"
loaf of bread	= phonogram: "t"; and ideogram: "female"

"MUT NETCHER" ("Mother of the god")

vulture	= phonogram: "m...t" ("vulture" and "mother" are homophones, pronounced alike)
flag	= ideogram: "god"; and phonogram: "n...t...r"
loaf of bread	= phonogram: reinforces "t"

"NEBET PET" ("Mistress of Heaven")

basket	= phonogram: "n...b" (homophone of word for "master")
loaf of bread	= phonogram: "t"; and ideogram: "female"
sky	= ideogram: "heaven"; and phonogram: "p...t"

(*Left*) Over 700 hieroglyphs made up the complex writing system. Only scribes and a few pharaohs were among the literate elite.

(*Above*) A copy from a thirteenth century B.C. inscription in the temple of Ramses II at Thebes. The pictures say, "Aset, great female, mother of the god, mistress of heaven."

Egyptian hieroglyphs were used until A.D. 394. They finally gave way (along with the Egyptian hieratic and demotic) to Greek after Alexander's conquest. The hieroglyphic system was left undeciphered for almost two millennia until the discovery of the trilingual Rosetta Stone in Egypt, and eventual translation by linguist Jean François Champollion.

There are only two powers in the world, the sword and the pen; and in the end the former is always conquered by the latter.
—Napoleon Bonaparte

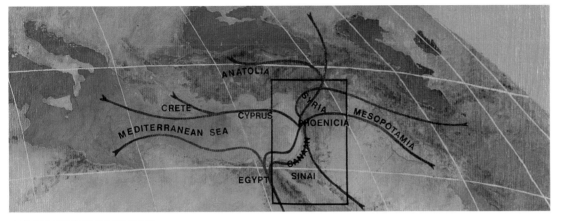

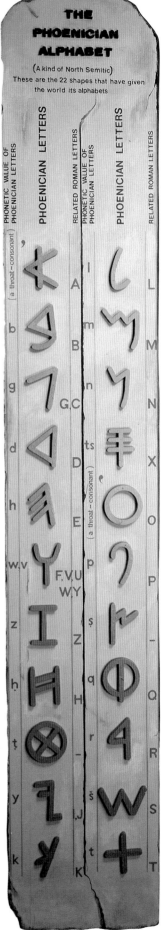

THE
PHOENICIAN
ALPHABET

(A kind of North Semitic)
These are the 22 shapes that have given
the world its alphabets

THE FIRST TRUE ALPHABET

As the great early civilizations of the Bronze Age began to fade and ordinary people needed to read and write, something new appeared: the first true alphabet.

Between 1800 B.C. and 1300 B.C., the alphabet was developed by the Semitic people living at the crossroads of the ancient world among a constant flow of merchandise, cultures, and ideas (*see map*). All the known writing systems criss-crossed here. At the same time, there was a demand for an easier way of writing.

The genius of the original Semitic alphabet maker lay in his selecting one method, that of symbolizing single speech sounds, and rejecting the other methods of the combination systems. From that eventually grew a variety of other alphabets.

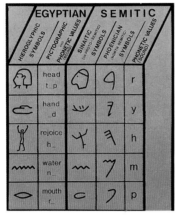

EGYPTIAN			SEMITIC		
HIEROGLYPHIC SYMBOLS	PICTOGRAPHIC	PHONETIC VALUES	SINAITIC (or PROTO-SEMITIC) SYMBOLS	PHOENICIAN (NORTH SEMITIC) SYMBOLS	PHONETIC VALUES (SOUND)
	head r_p				r
	hand _d				y
	rejoice h_				h
	water n_				m
	mouth r_				p

[*Above*] The inventors of the Semitic alphabet appear to have borrowed the shapes of some Egyptian hieroglyphs, but used them strictly as alphabet letters to represent speech sounds. They used some to represent the same sounds they had in Egyptian, others they used to represent the first sound of the Semitic word. All were consonants.

An ideographic system would need as many symbols as there are ideas to be expressed. (There has never been a true writing system that has been purely ideographic.) A phonographic system, however, needs only as many symbols as there are speech sounds for a particular language, usually about 30.

In the early Phoenician alphabet (*right*) notice that (1) the original version was all consonants; (2) the original alphabetical order has come down to us almost intact; (3) the Roman alphabet letters have retained the shapes of the originals to a remarkable degree, although the sound values of some have changed.

[*Top*] Ideographic writing represents ideas directly, paralleling the representation of ideas by spoken language, and not depending on it.
[*Bottom*] Phonographic, or alphabetic, writing represents ideas indirectly, by representing the speech sounds that mediate between ideas and a particular spoken language.

Who without books assays to learn, draws water in a leaky urn.

—Anon.

Boustrophedon in action— inspiration for early direction for writing.

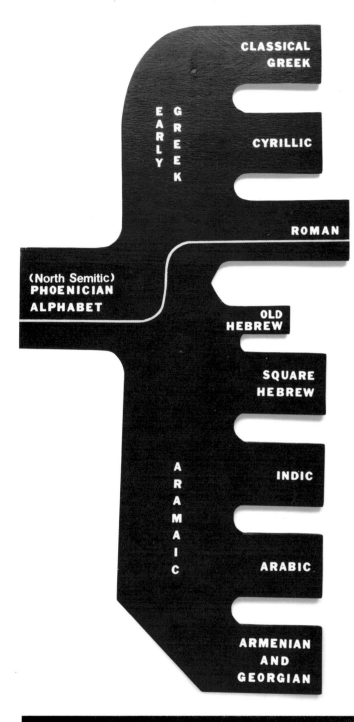

THE EARLY GREEK ALPHABET 850 B.C.
HOW EARLY GREEKS SOLVED THE VOWEL PROBLEM

The lack of vowels in the original alphabet became a problem for the rest of the world that inherited it. Most languages need to have their vowels written.

Semitic languages, such as Phoenician, Hebrew, and Arabic, though spoken with vowels, do not need them written to be intelligible.

However, Phoenicians sometimes indicated vowels for clarity. To do this they used certain consonants as a type of vowel:

V or W (Y) for "u" or "o"

Y (⅄) for "i"

They thought of them as *reading aids*; we call them *semivowels*.

The Phoenicians often spelled the name *David* as *Dvyd*, instead of just *Dvd*, to assure correct identification. Read from right to left:

Δ ⅄ Y Δ

D Y V D

The Phoenicians taught the Greeks to read and write with their all-consonant alphabet. But since written Greek could not be understood without vowels, *W* and *Y* were used extensively.

After the Greeks had assigned Semitic consonant letters to write their own consonant sounds, they proceeded to assign the leftover consonant letters to write their vowel sounds. There were only five leftovers:

Phoenician Consonants		Greek Vowels
⟨ ('alef)	=	A (alpha)
⟩ (he)	=	E (epsilon)
⋏ (yodh)	=	I (iota)
O ('ayin)	=	O (omicron)
Y (waw)	=	U (upsilon)

Later, the Greeks realized they needed more vowel letters and added H (ēta) and Ω (omega), but this was too late to influence the Roman alphabet, which had already adopted the five-vowel Greek alphabet. That is why we write the 14 English vowel sounds with only five letters.

EARLY PHOENICIAN ALPHABET

different letter shapes of the EARLY GREEK ALPHABET, each Greek City-State had its own variety

phonetic value of the Greek letters

a   b   g   d   e   v,w   z   h,ē   th   i   k   l   m   n   ks (x)   o   p   s   q   r   s   t   u,ü   ph,f   ks,kh   ps   ō

"As-the-ox-turns-in-ploughing"

(the Greeks called it "boustrophedon" = bou = ox, strophedon = turning)

This was a way of writing in ancient Greece — back and forth. Notice how the E's and K's get turned around, in alternate lines.

This seems to have been what got our letters turned around and headed in the opposite direction from the way the Phoenicians had originally written them. ⅃→E И→N ⅄→K

But in those days it didn't make much difference which way a letter faced, or even if it stood on its head! ∀ Ȿ A Ɑ (our letter A is an ox-head turned upside-down)

And the line of writing could climb up and down,

or go around

as easily as run horizontally in either direction.

Nothing was "standard" until Athens got the upper hand of the city states and standardized letter-shapes, direction of writing, and the direction a letter faced. They liked the left-to-right better than the other directions. And that's what was passed on to us.

→ ΚΕΝΑΡΙΟΝΤΙΑΣΕΝΙΚΕ →

Great things are done when men and letters meet;
These are not done by jostling in the street.

—R.S. Pittman (with apologies to Wm. Blake)

THE ETRUSCAN ALPHABET 800 B.C.
THE BRIDGE FROM GREEK TO ROMAN

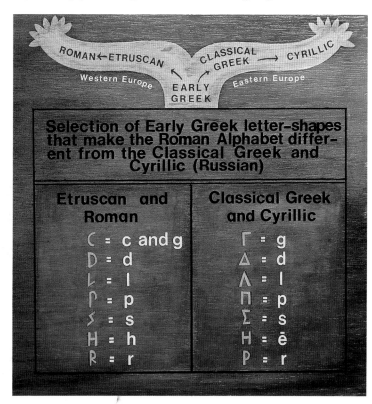

The Etruscans, the real developers of the Roman alphabet, dominated the Italian peninsula before the Romans came to power. They brought the early Greek alphabet to Italian soil in pre-Roman days, choosing certain letter shapes and changing a few sound values, to write their language. The Romans, in turn, took over the Etruscan alphabet for writing Latin, and passed it on to all Western European languages, including English.

Selection of Early Greek letter-shapes that make the Roman Alphabet different from the Classical Greek and Cyrillic (Russian)

Etruscan and Roman	Classical Greek and Cyrillic
C = c and g	Γ = g
D = d	Δ = d
L = l	Λ = l
P = p	Π = p
S = s	Σ = s
H = h	H = ē
R = r	P = r

A B C D E F G
N O P Q R S T U

THE ROMAN ALPHABET
650 B.C. STANDARD CAPITALS FOR WESTERN EUROPE

As Rome became a world empire, it assimilated the achievements of the peoples it conquered, especially the Greeks. These it spread from Britain to Egypt and from the Atlantic to Mesopotamia.

Most of the peoples Rome conquered had unwritten languages. With the spread of Christianity came the need to translate the Bible into other languages, requiring the adaptation of alphabets. One of the first of these was Visigoth.

The form of the Roman capital letters reflects the tools and techniques used making them:

1. The "thick and thin" quality and gradation of curves resulted from first drawing the letters on the stone with a wide flat lettering implement.

(*Below*) Roman writing tablet of beeswax and writing stylus.

(*Top*) The earliest-known example of the Etruscan alphabet, from the *Marsiliana Tablet,* about 700 B.C.

Most of the ten thousand examples of Etruscan writing in existence are on gravestones, with little more than a name.

The one shown here is typical. It says: *Vel Sethre Puia-C,* "Vel Sethre and Wife."

A little-known people, the Etruscans left behind a great heritage.

K L M

V X Y Z

(below) The Roman letters reached a standard of form that is still highly admired by printers and calligraphers. The favorite example is the inscription on the base of the Trajan Column in Rome, engraved A.D. 113.

Stone-cutter's chisel followed drawn letters exactly. "Serifs" popped either from the brush or the chisel's finishing touches ends of the strokes.

(Above) A copy of a portrait of Terentius Neo and his wife, a literate Roman couple, from a Pompeian wall painting before A.D. 79.

(Right) Ulfilas, Visigoth alphabet maker and Bible translator.

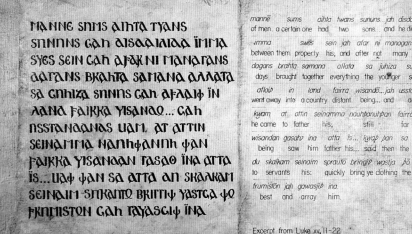

MANNE	SUMS	AIHTA TWANS	SUNUNS... JAH DISDAILIDA
manne	sums	aihta twans	sununs... jah disdailida
of men.	a certain one	had two	sons... and he divided

SNNNS GAH AISAAIAIAA INNA
imma ... *swēs* ... *sein jah afar ni managans*
between them ... property ... his; and after not ... many

SYES SEIN GAH AFAR NI MANATANS
dagans brahta samana ... *allata sa juhiza sunus jah*
days brought together ... everything the younger son and

AATANS BRAHTA SAMANA AAAATA
aflaiþ in iand fairra wisandō... jah usstandands
went away into a country distant being... and arising

SA GNHIZA SNNNS GAH AFAAIÞ IN
kwam at attin seinamma nauhþanuhþan fairra
he came to father his; still far

AANA FAIRKA YISANAQ... GAH
wisandan gasahv ina atta is... kwaþ þan sa atta
being saw him father his... said then the father

NSSTANAANAS UAM. AT ATTIN
du skalkam seinaim sprautō bringiþ wastja þō
to servants his: quickly bring ye clothing the

SEINAMMA NANHÞANNH ÞAN
frumistōn jah gawasjiþ ina.
best and array him.

FAIRKA YISANAAN TASAO INA ATTA

IS...UAÞ ÞAN SA ATTA AN SKAAKAM

SEINAIM STKANTO BRIITIÞ YASTGA ÞO

FRNMISTON GAH TAYASGIÞ INA

Excerpt from Luke xv, 11–22

THE VISIGOTH (GOTHIC) ALPHABET

The Visigoths, or West Goths, a warlike people, lived along the Roman frontier west of the Black Sea. After they had been "Christianized," Ulfilas (311-382), their bishop, saw they needed the Bible in their own tongue "to speak to their hearts."

First Ulfilas had to make an alphabet. He knew that neither the Greek nor the Roman alphabet would fit a Germanic language. He chose from these alphabets only the letters that corresponded to the speech sounds of Visigoth. For sounds for which there were no letters, he used runes, an early Germanic alphabet of limited use. With this, he translated the Bible.

The Visigoths migrated west and were the first to conquer Rome (A.D. 410). Their aim, however, was not so much to destroy but to acquire the benefits of civilization. It was largely due to the work of Ulfilas that these plunderers became peacemakers.

21

THE DEVELOPMENT OF THE ROMAN LOWERCASE ALPHABET

The Roman capital letters have come down to us unchanged. Roman lowercase letters evolved from the capitals, as a result of writing rapidly with pen and ink. Writing on wax tablets also had an influence.

The reproduction here is of a Latin message in Roman cursive script, scratched on a wax tablet. Transcribed and translated, it is:

Rufus callisuni salutem
Rufus, son of Callisunus, greetings
Epillico et omnibus
to Epillicus and all
contubernalibus certiores vos esse
his fellows

Square capitals were copied from the carved Roman capitals. The Rustic, Uncials, and Semi-Uncials each marked a step toward lowercase letter shapes.

Notice the stages of development for the letter *e*:

E ℇ e e

Each nationality developed a distinctive style. The Irish exerted the most influence on later styles.

The English variety of the Irish, taken to the continent, influenced the development of both the rounded Carolingian, named after Charlemagne, and the angular Gothic.

When printing was developed, the Gothic and an Italian revival of Carolingian, called Renaissance, became popular.

This latter style has continued as the Roman lowercase alphabet.

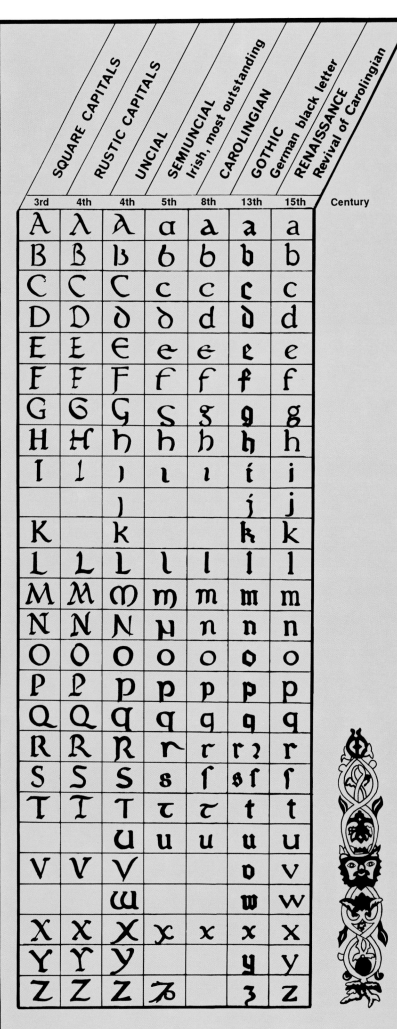

SQUARE CAPITALS	RUSTIC CAPITALS	UNCIAL	SEMIUNCIAL Irish, most outstanding	CAROLINGIAN	GOTHIC German black letter	RENAISSANCE Revival of Carolingian
3rd	4th	4th	5th	8th	13th	15th
A	λ	λ	α	a	a	a
B	B	b	b	b	b	b
C	C	C	c	c	c	c
D	D	ð	ð	d	d	d
E	E	E	e	e	e	e
F	F	F	f	f	f	f
G	G	G	S	ʒ	g	g
H	H	h	h	h	h	h
I	I	)	ı	ı	i	i
		)			j	j
K		k			k	k
L	L	L	l	l	l	l
M	M	m	m	m	m	m
N	N	N	ɲ	n	n	n
O	O	O	o	o	o	o
P	P	p	p	p	p	p
Q	Q	q	q	q	q	q
R	R	R	r	r	r ?	r
S	S	S	s	ſ	sſ	ſ
T	T	T	τ	τ	t	t
		u	u	u	u	u
V	V	V			v	v
		w			w	w
X	X	X	x	x	x	x
Y	Y	y			y	y
Z	Z	Z	ʒ		ʒ	z
						Century

22

And you shall write very clearly all the words of this law . . .
Deuteronomy 27:8

ALCUIN OF YORK
A.D. 730-804

After the fall of Rome, Western Europe lapsed into illiteracy. Kings could not read; bishops could not spell. Learning retreated to the monasteries, where monks made endless copies of books, all by hand.

Writing became chaotic. One monk could not read what another had written but copied it anyway. The text of even the Latin Bible was becoming distorted.

Charlemagne (Charles the Great) was deeply concerned. In A.D. 781, he invited Alcuin, an English scholar and churchman, to come and help.

At Charlemagne's orders, Alcuin set up a school that all monks attended. He set the following standards for writing:
1. Uniform spelling;
2. The Carolingian style of well-formed lowercase letters;
3. Capitals to begin a sentence and lowercase to continue;
4. Space between words;
5. Standard punctuation;
6. Division into sentences and paragraphs.

These standards are still our writing and printing conventions today.

Anglo-Saxon Runic alphabet

Anglo-Irish (or *Insular*) Roman alphabet, lower case

ic næfre þin wif .
I never   *thine wife,*

forðan þen ic
because   *I*

sýlfwýlles   eom   criste   gehalgod.
by my own will   *am*   *to Christ*   *hallowed.*

Text excerpt using Irish-style Roman alphabet

ALPHABETS FOR ENGLISH

RUNIC ALPHABET

The first "Englishmen," Germanic Anglo-Saxons, wrote with *runes.* These were derived from an Etruscan-related alphabet, fitted to Germanic languages, and styled for carving into wood. The Old English runic writing above (c. A.D. 650-700) says: ROMWALUS AND REUM-WALUS TWOEGEN, "Romulus and Remus twins."

ROMAN ALPHABET

About the time Christianity was introduced in England (c. A.D. 600), an Irish-style Roman alphabet was adapted.

In the eleventh-century excerpt (*right*), notice the adjustments that were made due to a shortage of letters in the Roman alphabet. For example, two runes were used for non-Latin sounds:

þ = *th* in þin, *thine*
p = *w* in pıf, *wife*

A letter was added, made from *d:*

ð = *th* (in forðan, *because*)

Joining *a* and *e* made:

æ (as in næfre, *never*)

Another combination was:

eo (as in eom, *am*)

The letter *y* was used as a vowel:

ẏ (as in rẏlf, *self*)

and *h* and *g* (ð) were each used for more than one sound.

In John Wycliffe's English Bible, (late fourteenth century), the rune þ (þ) was still used for *th*, but not the p for *w.* By then, *w* (w), "double-u," had been invented. The passage (*above*), from John 1:1-3, reads:

"In the bigynnyng was the word and the word was at God, and God was the word. This was in the bigy nyng at God. All thingis weren maad bi hym."

24

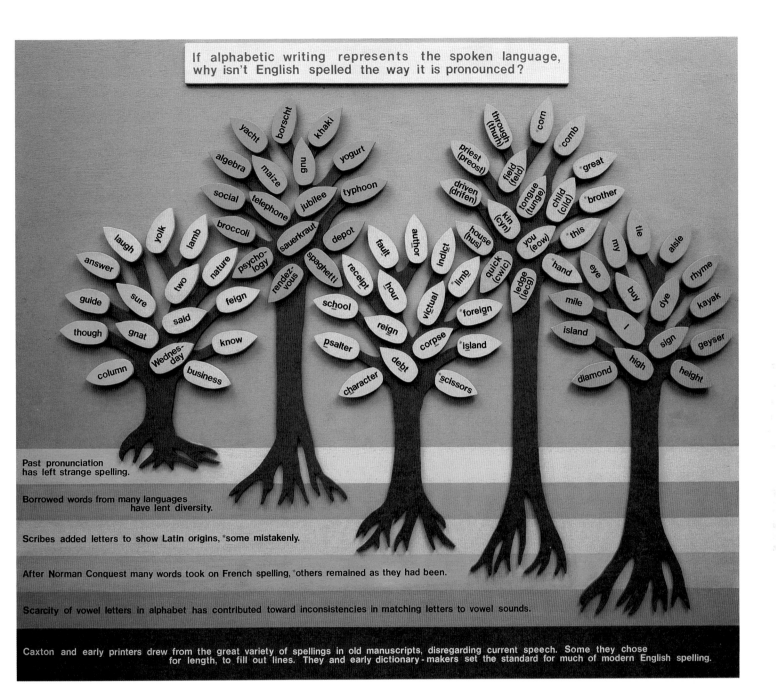

If alphabetic writing represents the spoken language, why isn't English spelled the way it is pronounced?

Past pronunciation has left strange spelling.

Borrowed words from many languages have lent diversity.

Scribes added letters to show Latin origins, *some mistakenly.

After Norman Conquest many words took on French spelling, *others remained as they had been.

Scarcity of vowel letters in alphabet has contributed toward inconsistencies in matching letters to vowel sounds.

Caxton and early printers drew from the great variety of spellings in old manuscripts, disregarding current speech. Some they chose for length, to fill out lines. They and early dictionary-makers set the standard for much of modern English spelling.

ENGLISH SPELLING: GOOD OR BAD?

In spite of well-known problems, there is reason and merit in English spelling. For example, in each pair of words below, identical spelling of the root, in spite of difference in pronunciation, helps readers grasp meaning:

> *extreme, extremity*
> *compose, composite*
> *critical, criticize*

Of course, many words show no such pattern.

The diversity in English spelling makes it comparable to Chinese, where one needs to memorize the form of each word. Though this can be difficult, some see it as a benefit. Those who have learned to read English will never confuse:

> *write, wright, right,* and *rite.*

Though they are pronounced the same, they have distinct meanings.

Admittedly, those who are content with the irregularities of English spelling are not thinking about children or speakers of another language struggling to learn English.

(*Right*) For the benefit of newcomers to English, William Cameron Townsend once produced a book of homophones. With a foreword by Dr. Olga Akhmanova of the University of Moscow, the introductory information reads: "Compiled ~~buy bye~~ by William Cameron Townsend and others who ~~no~~ know ~~sum~~ some of the ~~ruff~~ rough problems ~~eue yew~~ you ~~fined~~ find in English ~~dew do~~ due ~~two too~~ to homophones."

$1.00

Handbook of Homophones

(General American English)

Word pairs that are pronounced the same but differ in spelling and meaning

Compiled by
William Cameron Townsend
Summer Institute of Linguistics
Foreword by
Dr. Olga Akhmanova
University of Moscow

THE DEVELOPMENT OF PRINTING
JOHANNES GUTENBERG INVENTS MOVABLE TYPE

I know what I want to do: I wish to manifold (print) the Bible.
—Johannes Gutenberg

Johannes Gutenberg (1400-1468) looked for a better way to make books than copying by hand. He drew together elements from many trades.

Noting coin punches, he carved *letter punches* as molds for casting quantities of identical type. Then, as with block printing, he joined the type into page-sized galleys to be inked and printed. But unlike wood blocks, the type came apart for reassembling, to spell out any word.

He converted a wine press so that it would press pages onto the type. This was far superior to the old method of rubbing.

Oil-painting technology yielded ink; metallurgical developments provided alloys. Paper was becoming more

available. Bringing all these components together, Gutenberg created the first practical means of printing in the West.

Although Gutenberg is generally credited with the invention of movable type in the West, Laurens Coster of the Netherlands was probably the first European to make type—in 1440. However, cutting each by hand, instead of casting them in molds, made the process too time-consuming for mass production of books.

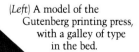

(*Left*) A model of the Gutenberg printing press, with a galley of type in the bed.

(*Above*) A facsimile sheet from Gutenberg's Latin Bible (1455), the first major book printed in Europe from movable type cast in molds.

The excellence of this work shows how well the problems of printing had been solved. Artists filled in initial letters and decorations to imitate handwritten books.

The Gothic or *black-letter* handwriting style of the Roman alphabet was copied for the metal type. It had evolved from the Carolingian and was popular in Northern Europe.

In Germany, Gothic (*Fraktur*) continued as the common style until 1941. The Old English and other varieties still have certain uses today.

Of making many books there is no end . . .
— Ecclesiastes 12:12

THE CLASSICAL GREEK ALPHABET 403 BC

UPPER CASE	Α Β Γ Δ Ε Ζ Η Θ Ι Κ Λ Μ Ν Ξ Ο Π Ρ Σ Τ Υ Φ Χ Ψ Ω	
LOWER CASE	α β γ δ ε ζ η θ ι κ λ μ ν ξ ο π ρ ς τ υ φ χ ψ ω	
PHONETIC VALUE	a b g d e z ē th i k l m n x o p r s t u,y f ch ps ō	

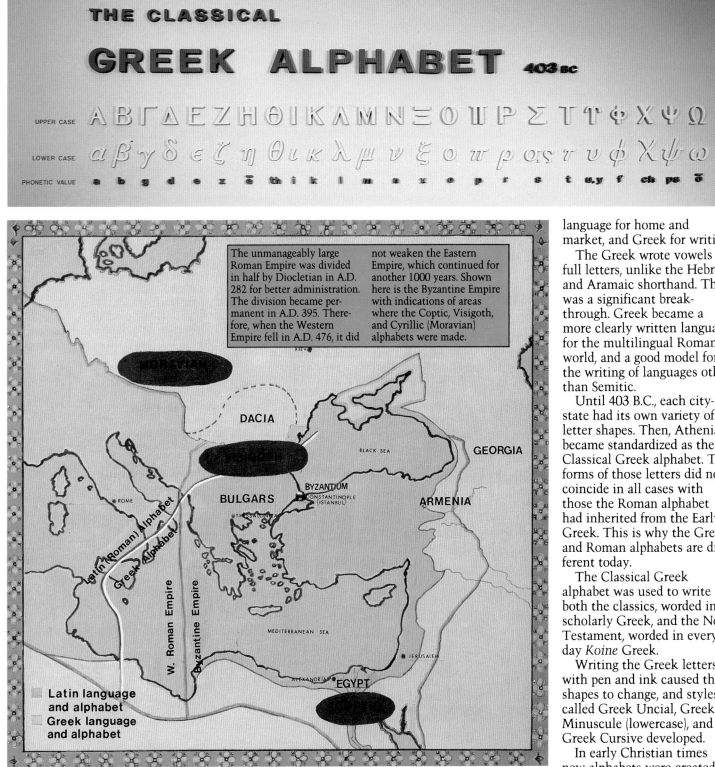

The unmanageably large Roman Empire was divided in half by Diocletian in A.D. 282 for better administration. The division became permanent in A.D. 395. Therefore, when the Western Empire fell in A.D. 476, it did not weaken the Eastern Empire, which continued for another 1000 years. Shown here is the Byzantine Empire with indications of areas where the Coptic, Visigoth, and Cyrillic (Moravian) alphabets were made.

Latin language and alphabet

Greek language and alphabet

Greece had become part of the Roman Empire in 146 B.C. Though Rome won political control, the prestige of the Greek language and literature kept Greek in the ascendancy until well into the Christian era.

This facilitated the spread

	WESTERN ROMAN EMPIRE	EASTERN ROMAN (BYZANTINE) EMPIRE
Capital	Rome	Byzantium (Constantinople, Istanbul)
Church	Roman Catholic	Greek Orthodox
Language	Latin	Greek
Alphabet	Latin (Roman)	Greek

of Greek translations of the Old Testament and, later, the distribution of the New Testament in its original Greek.

Jesus and the Jewish people of his day used several languages: Hebrew as their spoken religious language, the closely related Aramaic as the language for home and market, and Greek for writing.

The Greek wrote vowels as full letters, unlike the Hebrew and Aramaic shorthand. This was a significant breakthrough. Greek became a more clearly written language for the multilingual Roman world, and a good model for the writing of languages other than Semitic.

Until 403 B.C., each city-state had its own variety of letter shapes. Then, Athenian became standardized as the Classical Greek alphabet. The forms of those letters did not coincide in all cases with those the Roman alphabet had inherited from the Early Greek. This is why the Greek and Roman alphabets are different today.

The Classical Greek alphabet was used to write both the classics, worded in scholarly Greek, and the New Testament, worded in everyday *Koine* Greek.

Writing the Greek letters with pen and ink caused their shapes to change, and styles called Greek Uncial, Greek Minuscule (lowercase), and Greek Cursive developed.

In early Christian times new alphabets were created from the Greek Uncial for the purpose of translating the Bible into other languages, including Coptic (Egyptian), Visigoth (Germanic), and Cyrillic (Slavic).

The Armenian and Georgian alphabets were also influenced by the Greek Uncial.

THE CYRILLIC ALPHABET
TAILOR-MADE FOR SLAVIC LANGUAGES

W e don't understand Latin or Greek. Please send us someone to teach us in our language."

This was the message Prince Rostislav of the Slavic-speaking Moravians (of central Czechoslovakia) sent to the Byzantine emperor at Constantinople in A.D. 861.

Rostislav asked the Byzantine Church for assistance because they taught each nation in its own language, while the Church of Rome, at the time, used only Latin.

The emperor sent two Greek brothers, Cyril and Methodius, who knew both Slavic and Greek, to translate the Bible and liturgy. Two alphabets emerged (which Cyril himself may or may not have created). One soon fell into disuse.

The Cyrillic alphabet is a masterful piece of work, based on the Greek with borrowings from the Coptic and Hebrew.

According to tradition, the Apostle Andrew had introduced the Scyths, Sarmatians, and Slavs to the Christian faith on the hills of Kiev in the Ukraine. Some eight centuries later, it is said, Methodius went to Kiev and founded a great center of learning. He took with him the Bible which he and Cyril had translated, and introduced it and the Cyrillic alphabet to the Russians.

THE RUSSIAN CYRILLIC ALPHABET

Russian linguists have devised Cyrillic-type alphabets for many non-Slavic languages of the U.S.S.R. that had been unwritten or written with other alphabets. Pictured on the map are speakers of some of these languages: Yakut, Uzbek, Turkmen, Tadzhik, Kazakh, Kirghiz, Buryat, and others.

Today more than 200 million people, representing more than 100 languages, communicate nationally using the Cyrillic alphabet.

The Roman alphabet continues to be used for Latvian, Lithuanian and Estonian. Armenian and Georgian are written in their own alphabets.

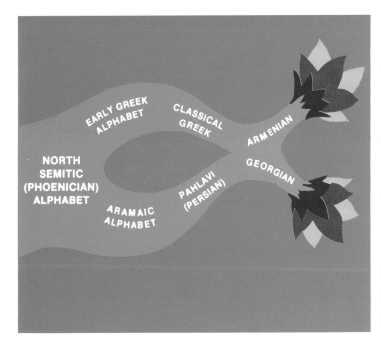

(*Above*) The Cyrillic alphabet for the Russian language—showing uppercase, lowercase, and phonetic value. Cyrillic alphabets are used for many other languages as well. (*Right*) The Gospel of John, printed before the

1918 revision of the Cyrillic alphabet, brought some letter shapes close to the Roman alphabet. (*Far Right*) A replica of a page from the Gospel of Matthew in the Church Slavonic language, using the early Cyrillic alphabet.

30

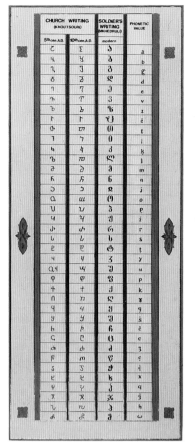

CHURCH WRITING (KHOUTSOURI)		SOLDIER'S WRITING (MKHEDRULI)	PHONETIC VALUE
5th cen A.D.	10th cen A.D.	modern	
Ⴀ	Ⴑ	ა	a
Ⴁ	Ⴔ	ბ	b
Ⴂ	Ⴃ	გ	g
Ⴃ	Ⴄ	დ	d
Ⴄ	Ⴅ	ე	e
Ⴅ	Ⴆ	ვ	v
Ⴆ	Ⴇ	ზ	z
Ⴈ	Ⴉ	თ	t
Ⴉ	Ⴊ	ი	i
Ⴊ	Ⴋ	კ	k
Ⴋ	Ⴌ	ლ	l
Ⴌ	Ⴍ	მ	m
Ⴍ	Ⴎ	ნ	n
Ⴎ	Ⴏ	ო	o
Ⴏ	Ⴐ	პ	p
Ⴐ	Ⴑ	ჟ	zh
Ⴑ	Ⴒ	რ	r
Ⴒ	Ⴓ	ს	s
Ⴓ	Ⴔ	ტ	t
Ⴔ	Ⴕ	უ	u
Ⴕ	Ⴖ	ფ	p
Ⴖ	Ⴗ	ქ	k
Ⴗ	Ⴘ	ღ	gh
Ⴘ	Ⴙ	ყ	q
Ⴙ	Ⴚ	შ	sh
Ⴚ	Ⴛ	ჩ	ch
Ⴛ	Ⴜ	ც	ts
Ⴜ	Ⴝ	ძ	dz
Ⴝ	Ⴞ	წ	ts
Ⴞ	Ⴟ	ჭ	ch
Ⴟ	Ⴠ	ხ	kh
Ⴠ	Ⴡ	ჯ	j
		ჰ	h
		ჵ	ō

THE GEORGIAN ALPHABET

The Georgians of the Caucasus area of the U.S.S.R. have an alphabet (*left*) which shows influences from the Greek, the Aramaic, and the Armenian alphabets.

One tradition credits Georgia's first king, Parnavaz, with its invention in the third century A.D.—to help unify his nation.

Another tradition is that Mesrop Mashtotz, after devising the Armenian alphabet in the fifth century A.D., did the same for Georgian.

С Т У Ф Х Ц Ч Ш Щ Ъ Ы Ь Э Ю Я
С Т У Ф Х Ц Ч Ш Щ Ъ Ы Ь Э Ю Я

s   t   u   f   kh   ts   ch   sh   shch   –   i   –   e   yu   ya

THE ARAMAIC ALPHABET

Aramaic, originally the language of Syria, was dominant in the Near East from about the fourth century B.C. through the sixth century A.D. The Aramaeans were caravan traders between the Mediterranean Sea and the Euphrates River. About 900 B.C. they began using the North Semitic alphabet to write their Semitic language. By 600 B.C. it had begun to differ from the parent alphabet (*right*).

Mongolian Alphabets grew from the Uighur-Sogdian-Aramaic (Central Asian) about A.D. 1250, and are used by Mongolians and others. Example:

Syriac Alphabets grew from the Aramaic about A.D. 100. They are used by groups of non-Jewish non-Islamic people of Near Eastern countries. Example:

Armenian and Georgian Alphabets, invented by Mesrop Mashtotz about A.D. 410 for translating the Bible, show influences from Persian (Pahlavi)-Aramaic and Greek alphabets.
Examples:
Armenian Հայկական ԱՆՁ
Georgian საქართველოს ᲨᲘᲜᲐ

Arabic Alphabets, grew from the Nabatean-Aramaic about 5th c. AD., perfected for writing the Koran, used by Islamic people in general. Example: سلطنة عمان

Square Hebrew Alphabet grew from the Aramaic about 450 BC. The Square Hebrew is used for writing the Old Testament, and for all purposes in Israel today. Example: ישראל

Indic (Brahmi) Alphabet, invented by Sanskrit linguists, 800-600 BC. for writing the Vedas, shows influence from the Aramaic. Daughter alphabets are used for many languages in and out of India.
Examples:
Devanagari मध्य प्रदेश
Telugu ఆంధ్రదేశము
Tibetan དབུས་གཙང་
Thai ประเทศไทย

ARAMAIC ALPHABET

Original location of Aramaeans
Assyrian Empire
Persian Empire

The Assyrians and Persians conquered the Aramaeans and resettled them. As a result, the Aramaic language replaced many others, becoming the common language from Egypt to India.

Likewise, the Aramaic alphabet replaced other writing systems, including cuneiform, and became the parent of most alphabets of Asia—over half the world's total.

Jesus' everyday speech was Aramaic. Parts of the Bible originally written in Aramaic include: Ezra 4:8 to 6:18, Daniel 2:4b to 7:28, and Jeremiah 10:11. Also some words and phrases of the New Testament were written in Aramaic, for example, *Talitha cumi, Maranatha,* and *Eli, Eli, lama sabaqtani.*

Mashtotz (*far right*) and Bishop Sahag invented the Armenian alphabet, translated the Bible, set up schools and spread Christianity. (*Opposite page, bottom*) A stylization of the Armenian alphabet with phonetic values for Eastern Armenia and (*last line*) Western Armenia.

DEVELOPMENT OF THE ARAMAIC ALPHABET

Sound Values	North Semitic 11th c. BC	Aramaic 8th c. BC	Aramaic 6th c. BC
' (a throat consonant, also vowel 'a')			
b			
g			
d			
h (also vowel 'e')			
w,v (also vowel 'u')			
z			
ḥ			
ṭ			
y (also vowel 'i')			
k			
l			
m			
n			
s			
' (a throat consonant)			
p			
ṣ			
q			
r			
s,sh			
t			

THE ARMENIAN ALPHABET

 King Tiridates accepted Christianity for his country in A.D. 301, making Armenia the first Christian nation. To translate the Bible, and thereby strengthen the Christian faith, Mesrop Mashtotz (354-439) wanted to develop an alphabet for Armenia. By this, he also hoped to preserve unity for this country, split between Greek and Persian rule.

Mashtotz had tried desperately to fit other alphabets to Armenian. Finally, in A.D. 406, he "received the alphabet in a heavenly vision." The alphabet shows influences from Greek and Pahlavi (Persian-Aramaic). A calligrapher finalized its form.

This alphabet and Bible allowed the church to develop independently. These have given moral fortitude through centuries of tribulation, and provided cultural identity in spite of worldwide dispersion.

The ink of the scholar is more sacred than the blood of the martyr.
—Mohammed

THE ARABIC ALPHABET

WRITING AS A FORM OF ART

The Roman and Arabic alphabets are cousins. Each has inherited different features of their North Semitic grandfather. For the Roman it is a similarity to Semitic letter shapes and the alphabetical order. For the Arabic it is the minimal use of vowel letters and the leftward direction of writing.

Arabic is a most efficient way of writing. It is stripped to the minimum: all styles are cursive and geared to rapid penwork, and most vowels are ignored.

The Arabic alphabet is one of the most important in the world. It is used by the followers of the Islamic faith —about 950 million people. Today's commercial developments in this area have brought this script into prominence in the rest of the world as well.

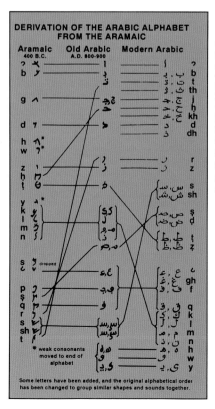

(*Above*) "In the name of God the Merciful, the Compassionate, the King of the Judgment Day, lead us to the Right Path."
(*Left*) In the course of time letters were added to Arabic, and the original alphabetical order was changed to group similar shapes and sounds together.

**FROM RIGHT TO LEFT,
THE COLUMNS SHOW THE LETTER-FORMS WHEN:**

4. NOT JOINED	(Phonetic Value)	3. JOINED ON THE RIGHT	2. JOINED ON BOTH SIDES	1. JOINED ON THE LEFT
	e,a			
	b			
	t			
	th			
	j			
	h			
	kh			
	d			
	dh			
	r			
	z			
	s			
	sh			
	ṣ			
	ḍ			
	ṭ			
	ẓ			
	gh			
	f			
	q			
	k			
	l			
	m			
	n			
	h			
	w,ū			
	y,ī			

blank spaces indicate that there is no special form

How can Semitic writing (Phoenician, Arabic, and Hebrew, etc.) function well when vowels are omitted?

It can because consonants and vowels have different roles in a Semitic language.

The root is a group of (usually) three consonants. The vowels spoken with the consonants are not part of the root:

KTB (*katab*) = write
KLB (*kalb*) = dog
WZN (*wazn*) = weigh

Each consonant group leads the reader to only one basic idea. There cannot be totally different meanings for one consonant group, as there are in English. For instance, in English, *HT* might be *hot, hate, hit, hut, hat,* or *hoot.*

Semitic vowels carry subsidiary information that can usually be gleaned from the context:

KaTaBa = he wrote
KuTiBa = it was written
KuTuB = books

So all three of these words can be written KTB (كتب) without ambiguity, in most contexts.

(*Left*) Most Arabic letters have four variant forms, the choice of which depends on where they fall: at the beginning or end of a word, within a word, or alone.

As the Dark Ages fell across Europe and the classics of Greece and Rome were being lost or destroyed, Muslim scholars continued to eagerly collect and translate them into Arabic.

Great universities were established at Islamic centers, where the classics and translations of works from many other cultures were studied. Notable contributions in mathematics, medicine and science were made at these centers. For many centuries the Islamic world carried the torch of civilization.

The European Renaissance resulted largely from the rediscovery of Europe's roots—preserved in the Arabic language and alphabet—and their translation back into Latin, the common language of European scholarship.

Islam disapproved of representing natural forms. This channeled creative endeavor in the Islamic world into other arts, the chief of which has always been calligraphy.

(*Left*) Examples of Arabic writing styles:

1, 2, 4, 6 and 7. Naskhi, the style most commonly used.

3. Thuluth, more elegant than Naskhi.

5. Kufic, an early monumental style no longer in common use.

9. Maghribi, with softer curves than Naskhi, favored in West Africa.

10. Nastiliq or Farsi, with words written on a slant, preferred in Iran and Pakistan.

(*Left*) A replica of a page from the Koran.
(*Below*) "God has blessed him and approved of him and has given him peace."

(*Below*) From Ghana, Africa, Muslim teacher's chart for teaching the Arabic alphabet and numbers 1—30 (read right to left). Pupils practice on a slate or board with soapstone or chalk.

Then the Lord said to Moses, "Write this on a scroll as something to be remembered..."

—Exodus 17:14

THE HEBREW ALPHABETS
SCRIPTS OF ISRAEL, OLD AND NEW

The Old Hebrew alphabet, "The Script of the Prophets," was doubtless that in which most of the Old Testament of the Bible was originally written. It was the same, or nearly the same, as the original North Semitic, with 22 letters—all consonants.

The modern Square Hebrew alphabet was developed from the Aramaic adaptation of the North Semitic alphabet.

The 22-letter set can be expanded by the addition of dots to change some consonants to others:

ב = v; בּ = b; שׁ = sh; שׂ = s; etc.

Five of the letters have two forms. In the pairs that follow those shown on the left are used at the end of words:

ך, כ = kh; ם, מ = m; ן, נ = n; etc.

The modern cursive (or handwriting) style is taken from Polish-German for Yiddish. There is no style of joined letters for written Hebrew.

MOSES AND THE FIVE SCRIPTS HE WOULD HAVE KNOWN

About the fifteenth century B.C., a Semitic authority standardized the form of the North Semitic alphabet. From earlier experiments in alphabet making, he determined letter shapes, phonetic value, and order. As to who that might have been, Moses lived at this time (see note on p. 39). Moses would have been familiar with at least five writing systems:

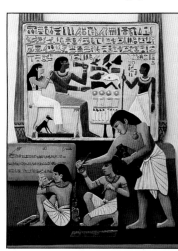

1. Egyptian hieroglyphics and hieratic writing. *"Moses was educated in all the learning of the Egyptians"* (Acts 7:21). Brought up as Pharaoh's grandson, Moses would have been taught Egyptian hieroglyphics—and the hieratic brush-and-ink style.

2. Babylonian cuneiform. *"...he was mighty in words and deeds."* (Acts 7:21). Moses, as a young diplomat in Pharaoh's court, would have used cuneiform. In his day, it was the dominant writing system for international correspondence.

3. Sinaitic (Proto-Semitic) alphabet. *"Moses fled and became an alien..."* (Acts 7:29). When Moses fled from Egypt, he came to Sinai. He certainly would have visited the nearby turquoise quarries, where there were inscriptions written in "sinaitic," an early experimental Semitic alphabet.

4. Canaanitic (Proto-Semitic) alphabet. *"...he led the flock, and came to the mountain of God."* (Exodus 3:1). When in Sinai, Moses probably came across broken pottery left by nomadic shepherds from Canaan with inscriptions in their type of alphabet. While tend-

ing sheep, he could have reflected on all these writing systems and might have perfected the North Semitic alphabet.

5. North Semitic alphabet. *"He gave to Moses...two tablets of stone, written with the finger of God"* (Exodus 31:18). Moses came down from Mt. Sinai with the tablets of the law, written in the North Semitic alphabet. This alphabet became established among the Hebrews through learning and copying the law. They may have passed it on to the Phoenicians, who distributed it to the rest of the world.

The dates of Moses are calculated as follows: I Kings 6:1 states that the Exodus took place 480 years before the fourth year of Solomon's reign. It is generally agreed that his reign began about 971 B.C. His fourth year would be about 967 B.C. Adding 480 to 967 gives 1447 B.C. for the Exodus. Acts 7:23 and 30 say that Moses was 80 years old at the time. He died at 120 years of age, according to Deuteronomy 34:7. Thus we arrive at 1527 to 1407 B.C. for Moses' dates.

(*Left*) The Ten Commandments (first part of each commandment) in the Square Hebrew alphabet.
(*Below*) A *Tenach* (Old Testament) scroll, as is used in the synagogue service. It is handwritten by a scribe on parchment (sheep skin). It has no vowel points.

A scroll was found . . . this was written on it . . .
— Ezra 6:2

Name of Letter	Tomb of Akhiram 1000 B.	Dead Sea Isaiah Scroll	Gezer Calendar 925 B.C.	Bar-Rekub Building Inscription 730 B.C.	Saqqara Papyrus 600 B.C.	Elephan-tine Papyrus 408 B.C.	Edfu Papyrus 275 B.C.	Uzziah Reburial Tablet A.D. 50	Bar-Kochba Letter A.D. 130	Poetic Fragment A.D. 350	Ben-Asher Codex A.D. 895	Printed Bible A.D. 1895
Kaf												
Lamed												
Mem												
Samekh												

THE DEAD SEA SCROLLS

When the Dead Sea Scrolls first came into the hands of scholars, one of the first questions they wanted answered was: "How old are the documents?"

After carefully unrolling the scrolls, scholars determined their ages by comparing their letter shapes with those of other documents whose age was already known.

On the "slide rule" (*above*) each horizontal row shows a particular letter of the Hebrew alphabet as it was written at various times during history. The slide is moved along until the letter shapes from the Dead Sea (Isaiah) Scroll form a transition between those to the left and right.

This analysis shows that the Isaiah Scroll can be dated between 275 B.C. and A.D. 50.

The Isaiah Scroll is over 1000 years older than the oldest copy of Isaiah previously known. The scroll has helped to verify the accuracy of the Old Testament text and to show how Judeo-Christian Scriptures have been faithfully preserved.

t,th	s	sh	r	q	ts	f	p	ʿ	s	n	m	l	kh	k	y	ṭ	ḥ	z	w,v	h	d	g	v	b	ʾ	phonetic values
ת	שׁ	שׂ	ר	ק	צ	פ	פ	ע	ס	נ	מ	ל	כ	כ	י	ט	ח	ז	ו	ה	ד	ג	ב	ב	א	the 22 basic letters + 4

word-final forms of letters
ץ ף ן ם ך

The Old Hebrew alphabet was either the original North Semitic or very similar to it. But when the Jews returned from Babylonian exile in 538 B.C., they had become accustomed to the Aramaic speech and alphabet.

Many Jews no longer understood Hebrew, so when Ezra the Scribe (about 450 B.C.) read the Hebrew scriptures to them, he translated into Aramaic.

"And they read from . . . the Law of God, translating to give the sense so that they understood the reading." (Nehemiah 8:8)

Ezra is credited with starting to write Hebrew with the square letter shapes, while using some features of Old Hebrew letters. (Notice transitional letter shapes along the slide rule, *above*.)

This was the origin of the present Hebrew alphabet. It eventually replaced the Old Hebrew alphabet for making copies of the Old Testament, and is the script of Israel today (*above*).

The modern Israeli Hebrew is like a new sprout from a very old stump. Hebrew had not been generally spoken since the days of Ezra. Now that it is the language and alphabet of Israel, decisions are being made as to how to write it.

Though for over 1600 years Hebrew had not been a commonly spoken language, it had continued to be written and read. Toward the end of the nineteenth century, Eliezer Ben-Yehudah (1858-1922) wanted to make Hebrew once more the language of the Jewish people. Gradually, others caught the vision, until Hebrew became the alphabet and language of modern Israel.

Never before had a language that had virtually died in antiquity been revived to become the common speech of a nation. However, the lack of words for the complexities of modern life was a problem.

A NEW TESTAMENT IN 12 LANGUAGES

This book (*above*) is one volume of the famous *Polyglot* New Testament by Elias Hutter, published in Nuremberg, Germany, in 1599.

Each verse is written in 12 languages: Greek, Syriac, Hebrew, Latin, German, Bohemian, Italian, Spanish, French, English, Danish, and Polish. Three entirely different alphabets have been used and several styles of some. The English used here is 12 years older than that in the King James Version of the Bible.

The Hebrew part, except for Matthew and the book of Hebrews, is the first translation of the New Testament into that language—the work of Hutter himself.

(*Above*) Ben-Yehudah wrote a dictionary and founded a language academy to deal with the problem of a lack of words for modern developments and concepts in Hebrew, a language revived after long disuse.

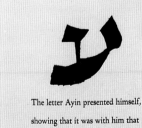

The letter Ayin presented himself, showing that it was with him that the word Anawah, humility, began. But the Lord, blessed be He, said unto him: "I cannot use you for the beginning of the world, for it is with you that the word Aerwah, immorality, begins."

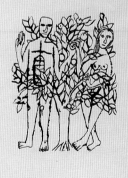

(*Left*) Artwork from *The Alphabet of Creation* by Ben Shahn.
(*Above*) An illustrated version of *Winnie the Pooh*, written in the Hebrew language.

My mission is to urge a world-wide commerce of heart and mind, sympathy and understanding.

—Rabindranath Tagore

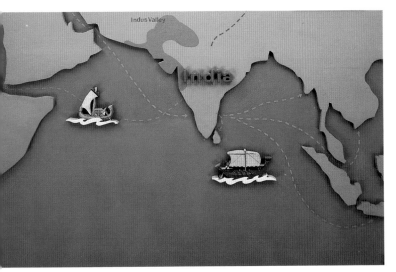

THE INDIC ALPHABETS
A NON-GREEK VOWEL SOLUTION FOR ASIA

After the Roman and Arabic alphabets, the Indic is the most extensively used in the world. It has spread to the countries around India and to southeast Asia.

The minor attention to vowels, inherited from the original Semitic alphabet, makes the Indic alphabets different from those of Europe.

Some scholars think that India's alphabets are derived from the ancient Indus Valley script—only partially deciphered. Others believe that India's parent alphabet, the Brahmi, was developed from the Early Aramaic as a result of sea trade between Babylon and India (800 to 600 B.C.).

If that is the case, some-thing like the above might have taken place. A Babylonian merchant explains alphabetic writing to a merchant from India: "You don't draw a picture of a ship, you say 'ship,' and you write a symbol for each way your mouth moves as you say it."

An Aramaic (North Semitic) origin for India's alphabets is postulated because (1) Semitic alphabets had no vowel letters and Indic alphabets give minimal attention to vowels (in spite of their great importance in India's spoken languages), and (2) they share some similar letter shapes.

Some Similar Letter-shapes of Aramaic (N. Semitic) and Brahmi (Indic) Alphabets					
NORTH SEMITIC	ARAMAIC about 600 B.C.	BRAHMI	EARLY SOUTH INDIC	EARLY NORTH INDIC	PHONETIC VALUE
ЖК	Қ	Я	Ч	Н	a
1	Λ	Λ	7	7	ga
Y	Y	ゟ	Ұ	⅄	va
⊕	Ꮾ	O	O	Θ	tha
∟	∟	Ս٨	Ս	ハ	la
₸ᛖ	५г	ѡ	↵	↵	sa
?	?	ᄂ	∟	Ч	pa
+.X	Xቦ	Λ	Ꮣ	ᆿ	ta
ᙡ	५.Ⴤ	Ϫ	Ⴤ	Ꮺ	ma

(*Above left*) An enlarged copy of an Indus seal. Carved in soapstone, these seals are about one inch square and often feature the image of an animal with an inscription, which had to be carved left to right be read right to left.

Various scripts on a variety of media (*clockwise from top right*): A hand written book in the Devanagari alphabet; a book in Oriya script on palm leaf pages (letters are etched with a metal stylus) a handwritten book in the Newari language of Nepal using Devanagari script; a handwritten book in the Tibetan alphabet.

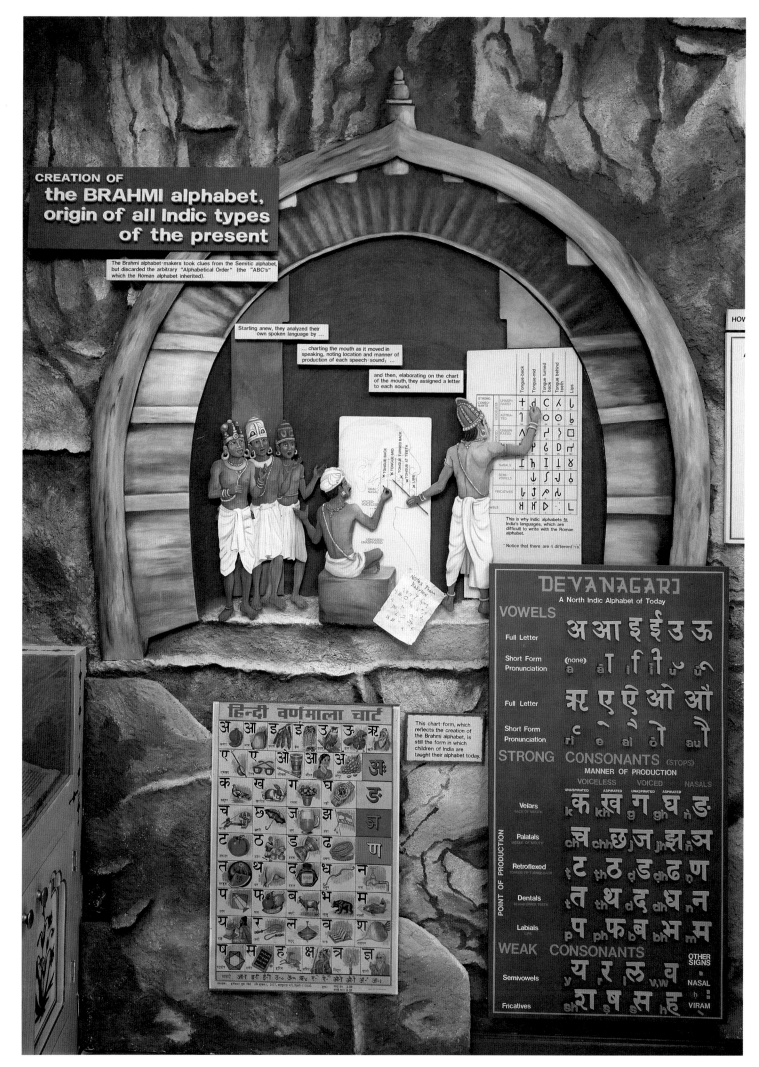

I ndia has one sixth of the total world population—over 800 million—representing many different cultures, languages, and alphabets.

The languages of North India are Indo-European, whereas the languages of South India are Dravidian, a large language family of the Southern portion of India. But

the alphabets of both North and South India are derived from the Brahmi.

North Indic alphabets like Devanagari feature straight strokes because the letters were originally carved in wood. South Indic alphabets like Telugu feature curves because the letters were etched on palm leaves. Straight lines would have slit the leaf.

The Brahmi alphabet developed into two main types: the Gupta, ancestor of North Indic alphabets; and the Grantha, ancestor of South Indic alphabets.

The Tibetan alphabet developed from the Gupta in the seventh century A.D. This, in turn, had an influence on the Mongolian and possibly the Korean alphabets.

The South Indic Grantha was taken to southeast Asia in the fourth or fifth century A.D. by Hindu priests and adventurers, and later, by Buddhists.

The Ethiopic alphabet also seems to have been influenced by the Indic in the matter of indicating vowels by small strokes added to the consonants.

T he world's original alphabet had only consonant letters. In India, as in Greece, vowel indications were added. In southeast Asia, it was necessary to write tones as well.

More than half the languages of the world are *tonal languages*. In these, besides consonants and vowels making distinctions between words, the pitch of the voice, rising and falling within the word, also distinguishes meaning.

For instance, in Thai the sound *my* has five different meanings, differentiated solely by its tone.
my with high tone = wood;
my with mid tone = much;
my with low tone = new;
my with rising tone = to mean;
my with falling tone = widow.

In English, intonation affects the meaning of a *sentence*. But in a tonal language, the level used with *each word* differentiates its meaning.

(*Above* and *left*) Religious leaders read pages from an Indic manuscript, while a monk carves a "page" for woodblock printing.

INDIC ALPHABETS
OF THE PHILIPPINES

From the ninth to the fifteenth centuries, the huge Javanese Empire stretched from Sumatra in the west, to the coast of New Guinea in the east, and up to the northern Philippines—an area larger than the United States.

A relic of this civilization is found in the Indic-type alphabets still used by some minority groups of the Philippines.

The major linguistic groups have used the Roman alphabet almost since Magellan first came to the Philippines in 1521. But a few language groups, living in remote areas, and without schools, continued their ancient Indic writing systems. Some have a literacy rate as high as sixty percent.

The Buhid writing (*above*) is scratched with a knife on a joint of green bamboo. True to Indic form, the alphabets consist mainly of consonants, and the "inherent" vowel sound *a*.

A mark above the consonant stands for *i* or *e*, and one below for *o* or *u*. Full vowel letters are used only if a vowel begins a word, or is the entire word. Syllable-final consonants are not written.

K ing Ramkhamhaeng adapted the Kampuchean alphabet, derived from South Indic, to the writing of Thai.

ฃ์ ธ ฮ น เ ขา น เอ์ ห่า น บ่

He indicated its three tones with the symbols (+), (|), and the absence of a mark. The marks indicated the actual tones used in pronouncing words.

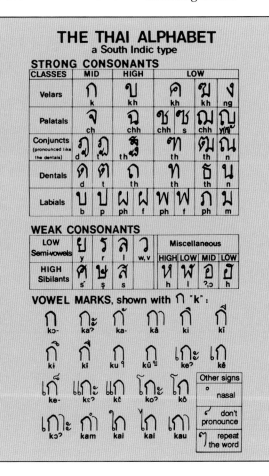

THE THAI ALPHABET
a South Indic type
STRONG CONSONANTS

CLASSES	MID	HIGH	LOW		
Velars	ก k	ข kh	ค kh	ฆ kh	ง ng
Palatals	จ ch	ฉ chh	ช chh	ซ s	ฌ chh / ญ y(n)
Conjuncts (pronounced like the dentals)	ฎ d / ฏ t	ฐ th	ฑ th	ฒ th	ณ n
Dentals	ด d / ต t	ถ th	ท th	ธ th	น n
Labials	บ b / ป p	ผ ph / ฝ f	พ ph / ฟ f	ภ ph	ม m

WEAK CONSONANTS

LOW Semi-vowels	ย y	ร r	ล l	ว w, v	Miscellaneous			
					HIGH	LOW	MID	LOW
HIGH Sibilants	ศ s'	ษ ṣ	ส s		ห h	ฬ l	อ ?,ɔ	ฮ h

VOWEL MARKS, shown with ก "k":

ก kɔ-	กะ ka-	ก้ ka-	กา kā	กิ ki	กี kī
กึ kï	กื kï	กุ ku	กู kū	เกะ ke?	เก kē
เก้ ke-	แกะ kɛ?	แก kɛ	โกะ ko?	โก kō	*Other signs* ◦ nasal
เกาะ kɔ?	กำ kam	ไก kai	ใก kai	เกา kau	่ don't pronounce / ๆ repeat the word

Syllables of the Buhid Alphabet
used on the joint of bamboo in the apparatus

basic consonant letters pronounced with "a"	consonants with added vowel-marks for:	
	"ı"	"o"
t	ᝦ	ᝦ̄	ᝦ
d	ᝧ	ᝧ̄	ᝧ
p,f	ᝨ	ᝨ	ᝨ
b	7	7̄	Ɫ
k	ᝣ	ᝣ̄	Ɫ
m	ᝪ	ᝪ̄	ᝪ
n	7/	7/	7Ɫ
ng	ᝠ	ᝠ	ᝠ
l	ᝮ	ᝮ̄	ᝮ
r	ᝲ	ᝲ	ᝲ
h	᝱	᝱	᝱
g	ᝬ	ᝬ̄	ᝬ
s	ᝳ	ᝳ̄	ᝳ
w	᝵	᝵̄	᝵
y	᝶		᝶
vowel-letters	ᝲ	ᝲ	ᝳ

THE MONGOLIAN ALPHABET

Kublai Khan, ruler of half the known world, in 1260 A.D. established an official alphabet for his empire.

He intended for it to serve all the languages from Austria right, unlike Chinese. Today this alphabet is used in the Mongolian People's Republic and Inner Mongolia. However, the Russian Cyrillic script was decreed the official alphabet of the former in 1950 and is used to teach reading and writing in the latter.

8

De Accentibus & alijs fignis in vocalibus.

CAPVT II.

Iximus accentus effe quafi animam uocabulorum in hoc idiomate, atque ideo fumma diligentia funt addifcendi. Vtimur ergo triplici accentu linguæ Græcæ, acuto, graui, & circumflexo, qui quia non fufficiunt, addimus iota fubfcriptum, & fignum interrogationis noftræ; nam toni omnes huius linguæ ad fex claffes reducuntur, ita ut omnes prorfus dictiones huius idiomatis ad aliquam ex his fex claffibus feu tonis pertineant, nulla uoce prorfus excepta.

Primus igitur tonus eft æqualis, qui fine ulla uocis inflexione pronunciatur, ut ba, res: quod ita uerum eft, ut etiamfi quis aliquem interroget per uocem, chang, quæ eft æqualis, ut cò chang, eft ne; nullo modo debeat inflectere uocem interrogando, quia uox interrogatiua, chang, nullo notatur accentu, quod fi inflecteretur uocis tonus, tunc effet alia fignificatio: uoces itaque quæ hunc æqualem habent tonum, nullo notantur accentu; & hoc eft fufficiens illarum diftinctiuum fignum, cùm omnes aliæ fuum accentum habeant.

Secundus tonus eft acutus, qui profertur acuendo uocẽ, & proferendo dictionem, ac fi quis iram demoftraret, ut ba concubina Regis, uel principis alicuius uiri.

Tertius eft grauis, & profertur deprimendo uocem, ut ba ania, uel Domina.

Quartus eft circumflexus, qui exprimitur inflectendo uocem ex imo pectore prolatam, & poftea fonarè eleuatam, ut ba colaphus, uel colaphizare.

Quintus uocatur ponderofus feu onerofus quia cum quodam pondere feu onere ex imo pectore prolata noce exprimitur, & notatur cum iota fubfcripto ut ba res derelicta.

Sextus

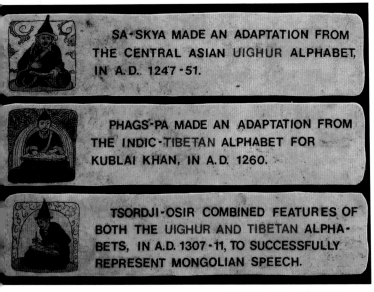

SA·SKYA MADE AN ADAPTATION FROM THE CENTRAL ASIAN UIGHUR ALPHABET, IN A.D. 1247·51.

PHAGS·PA MADE AN ADAPTATION FROM THE INDIC·TIBETAN ALPHABET FOR KUBLAI KHAN, IN A.D. 1260.

TSORDJI·OSIR COMBINED FEATURES OF BOTH THE UIGHUR AND TIBETAN ALPHABETS, IN A.D. 1307·11, TO SUCCESSFULLY REPRESENT MONGOLIAN SPEECH.

(*Above*) The Mongolian alphabet was the work of three Tibetan lamas.

to Korea—to unify his vast Mongolian Empire.

Kublai's grandfather, Genghis, had used the Uighur alphabet; but that needed modification for writing the Mongolian language. The Mongolian alphabet is a central Asian derivative of the Aramaic alphabet with influences from Indic-Tibetan.

The Mongolian script is written vertically, from top to bottom like Chinese, but columns proceed from left to

```
North Semitic
alphabet
        |
Aramaic
alphabet
   |
Pahlavi          Brahmi
(Persian         (Indic)
 or
Iranian)
   |
Sogdian
(Central
Asian)
   |
Uighur
(Central         Tibetan
Asian)
        |
Mongolian
alphabet
```

QUÔC NGƯ
A NEW DIMENSION FOR THE ROMAN ALPHABET

Vietnam was the only country of southeast Asia more influenced by China than by India, having been a province of China for over 1000 years. Only Chinese was written until, in the ninth century A.D., some Vietnamese wanted to write their literature in their own language. They adapted Chinese characters to Vietnamese, but in a haphazard way.

Nevertheless, this writing, called *Nôm*, or *Chú Nôm*, "script of the spoken language," was a way to write their own language.

Europeans began coming to Vietnam in the sixteenth century. To learn Vietnamese, they tried writing it in Roman alphabets.

A French Jesuit missionary, Alexandre de Rhodes, took these efforts and developed an efficient Roman-type alphabet for Vietnamese. Long before the days of descriptive linguistics, de Rhodes was aware of the prime importance of tone in the speech of these people.

At the turn of the twen-

tieth century, there were four writing systems in use in Vietnam: Chinese, Nôm, French, and de Rhodes'.

In the 1940s, there was a drive toward independence and literacy for everyone in the Vietnamese language. Only the de Rhodes alphabet, called *Quôc Ngư*, "national script," was found suitable. Today nearly all speakers of Vietnamese are literate in *Quôc Ngư*.

(*Above*) Father Alexandre de Rhodes of Vietnam. (*Top*) A page of de Rhodes' Vietnamese-Portuguese-Latin Dictionary. Note: the word *ba* has six different meanings, depending on tone. Five of them are circled here.

(*Below*) 1. King Solomon and the Queen of Sheba. 2. A priest with Frumentius' cross. 3. An ancient inscription in the Sabean South Semitic alphabet. 4. Some of the ethnic types of Ethiopia. 5. The rooftop of a church cut into living rock.

6. A cataract on the upper Nile in Ethiopia. 7. A religious procession. 8. A Bible portion in today's Amharic alphabet. 9. An Amharic man of Ethiopia. 10. Reading the ancient Ge'ez Bible. 11. University students of Ethiopia.

THE ETHIOPIC ALPHABET
INDIC VOWELS ON SOUTH SEMITIC CONSONANTS

About 500 B.C. Sabeans from South Arabia (Sheba) crossed the Red Sea and founded the Kingdom of Axum (now Ethiopia). They took with them their South Semitic all-consonant alphabet.

During the early fourth century A.D., the 22 consonants took on vowel indications for the seven vowel sounds of their Ge'ez lan-guage. They were written with small appendages to the consonant letters, with modifications of their shapes. This method of writing vowels is similar to that of Indic alphabets.

Tradition credits Frumentius with this change. He also introduced Christianity and translated the Bible into Ge'ez.

As a youth Frumentius had traveled to India where he may have noted Indic vowel writing. Shipwrecked on his return, he was taken to the king and ultimately became secretary-treasurer. In A.D. 333 he converted King Ezana to Christianity. Later, Frumentius was named Bishop of Ethiopia and estab-lished the national church. Frumentius' alphabet is still the national alphabet of Ethiopia.

(*Below*) Scraping hair off sheep skin for parchment, writing, and "powdering" ink to help it dry—ancient writing was a technology.

ANCIENT WRITING ACTIVITIES IN ETHIOPIA
a painting from Ethiopia

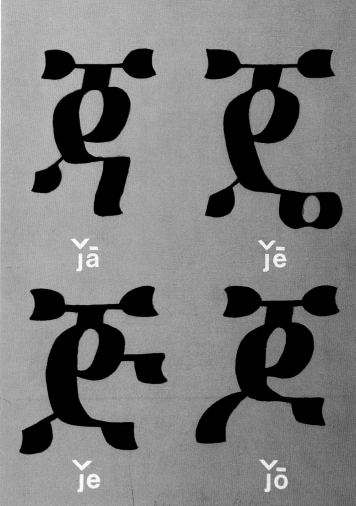

y̌jā y̌jē
y̌je y̌jō

(*Above*) Ethiopic syllable letters with their vowel indicators.
(*Right*) Because vowel indications modify the shapes of the consonant letters in such irregular ways, on the chart all syllables of the writing system are presented, rather than the consonants and vowels separately.

Presented as an alphabet, Amharic would have 37 consonant letters and seven vowel indications. However, here there are 251 characters.

The Ethiopic Alphabet called Ge'ez adapted to the modern Amharic language

basic forms of consonants, pronounced with "a"	ū	ī	ā	ē	e	ō
h	ሀ	ሁ	ሂ	ሃ	ሄ	ህ	ሆ
l	ለ	ሉ	ሊ	ላ	ሌ	ል	ሎ
ḥ	ሐ	ሑ	ሒ	ሓ	ሔ	ሕ	ሖ
m	መ	ሙ	ሚ	ማ	ሜ	ም	ሞ
š	ሠ	ሡ	ሢ	ሣ	ሤ	ሥ	ሦ
r	ረ	ሩ	ሪ	ራ	ሬ	ር	ሮ
s	ሰ	ሱ	ሲ	ሳ	ሴ	ስ	ሶ
*š	ሸ	ሹ	ሺ	ሻ	ሼ	ሽ	ሾ
q	ቀ	ቁ	ቂ	ቃ	ቄ	ቅ	ቆ
qw		ቈ		ቊ	ቋ	ቌ	ቍ
b	በ	ቡ	ቢ	ባ	ቤ	ብ	ቦ
t	ተ	ቱ	ቲ	ታ	ቴ	ት	ቶ
*ch	ቸ	ቹ	ቺ	ቻ	ቼ	ች	ቾ
ḫ	ኀ	ኁ	ኂ	ኃ	ኄ	ኅ	ኆ
hw		ኈ		ኊ	ኋ	ኌ	ኍ
n	ነ	ኑ	ኒ	ና	ኔ	ን	ኖ
*n´	ኘ	ኙ	ኚ	ኛ	ኜ	ኝ	ኞ
ʾ	አ	ኡ	ኢ	ኣ	ኤ	እ	ኦ
k	ከ	ኩ	ኪ	ካ	ኬ	ክ	ኮ
*ḥ´	ኸ	ኹ	ኺ	ኻ	ኼ	ኽ	ኾ
kw		ኰ		ኲ	ኳ	ኴ	ኵ
w	ወ	ዉ	ዊ	ዋ	ዌ	ው	ዎ
ʿ	ዐ	ዑ	ዒ	ዓ	ዔ	ዕ	ዖ
z	ዘ	ዙ	ዚ	ዛ	ዜ	ዝ	ዞ
*ž	ዠ	ዡ	ዢ	ዣ	ዤ	ዥ	ዦ
y	የ	ዩ	ዪ	ያ	ዬ	ይ	ዮ
d	ደ	ዱ	ዲ	ዳ	ዴ	ድ	ዶ
*j	ጀ	ጁ	ጂ	ጃ	ጄ	ጅ	ጆ
g	ገ	ጉ	ጊ	ጋ	ጌ	ግ	ጎ
gw		ጐ		ጒ	ጓ	ጔ	ጕ
ṭ	ጠ	ጡ	ጢ	ጣ	ጤ	ጥ	ጦ
ch	ጨ	ጩ	ጪ	ጫ	ጬ	ጭ	ጮ
p	ጰ	ጱ	ጲ	ጳ	ጴ	ጵ	ጶ
ṣ	ጸ	ጹ	ጺ	ጻ	ጼ	ጽ	ጾ
ḍ	ፀ	ፁ	ፂ	ፃ	ፄ	ፅ	ፆ
f	ፈ	ፉ	ፊ	ፋ	ፌ	ፍ	ፎ
*p	ፐ	ፑ	ፒ	ፓ	ፔ	ፕ	ፖ

* = additions for the Amharic language

SCRIPTS OF AFRICA

Africa, the 2nd largest continent, is the home of many interesting writing-systems, including
- one of the most ancient -- Egyptian Hieroglyphics;
- the only South Semitic of today -- Ethiopic;
- a purely African descendant of Phoenician --Tifinagh;
- and some modern originals.

It takes about three months for the Tuareg to cross the vast expanse of the Sahara (half the size of the United States). They transport gold, salt, ivory, and books to and from centers such as Timbuktu. Known as the veiled men of the desert, Tuareg men, not the women, veil their faces, considering it indecent to expose their mouths—even while eating.

DERIVATION OF TIFINAGH ALPHABET

Phoenician or Punic	Libyan or Numidian		Berber or Tifinagh	phonetic values
	horizontal	vertical		
				ʼ, a
				b
				g
				d
				h
				w, u
				z, ẓ
				ḥ
				ṭ, d
				y, i
				k, ḥ
				l
				m
				n
				s
				c, gh
				p, f
				q
				r
				s
				t

TIFINAGH

In 814 B.C., Elissa-Dido, perhaps a grandniece of the Biblical Jezebel, founded Carthage, the western capital of the Phoenicians. The Phoenician alphabet they used was called Punic.

In the second century B.C., the Semitic-Berber people of North Africa, called Numidians, built a mighty empire that transcended Carthage. They apparently adopted the Punic alphabet, adding some of their traditional symbols as letters.

The modern Tuaregs are descendants of the Numidians. Camel caravanners for a thousand years, they have dominated the trade routes of the Sahara. Tuaregs of Niger and Mali still use a Punic alphabet they call Tifinagh, meaning *characters*. They prefer it to the Arabic or the Roman alphabets.

VAI

The Vai writing system of Liberia was the first of several recently invented by native speakers to protect and promote their own cultures.

It was Momolu Duwalu Bukele who either invented the Vai script or transformed an ancient picto-ideographic system into a phonetic syllabary. In either case, it is a remarkable creation. He may have gotten the idea of a syllabary from a half-Cherokee, half-African man who settled in Vai country around the time the Cherokee alphabet was invented in 1821.

Progressively simplified, the present set of 212 symbols continues to be widely used in spite of the presence of the simpler Roman alphabet. Vai is used for correspondence, to codify edicts, to record traditional tales, to keep accounts, and for translations of the Bible.

THE MODERN VAI SYLLABARY

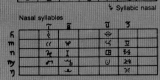

A syllabary is a writing system in which each letter represents a whole syllable. The Vai syllabary has been progressively simplified. The last vestiges of ideographs have been dropped.

BAMUN

Inspired by a dream, King Njoya of Cameroon asked his people to draw different objects and name them. With these he invented a script that was picto-ideographic, using a symbol for each word. From there, during King Njoya's lifetime, it progressed into a phonetic script.

Njoya used the *rebus* method of picturing a word for another that sounds the same, like a *nose* (ﾐ) for the word *knows*. This led to using symbols for their sounds as well as for their pictured meanings.

The king set up schools, or "book houses," where hundreds learned to read and write. Considerable literature was produced: official documents, histories, correspondence, and Bible translation. After Njoya's death in 1933, the syllabary gradually fell into disuse.

Development of Bamun Symbols

Early pictographic – about 1897

ngom sun	myt moon	membaa man	mamgbie name
li eye	vom belly	ngue snake	nyam horse

Later developments

phonetic value	Bamun word	meaning	1907	1911	1916	1918
fo, f	fom, mfon	king				
fè, f	fè	burn, work				
fa, f	fama	eight				
fou, f	fou	measure				
pwò, p	pwò	arms				
ña, n	ña	here				
mi, m	mi	face				
ku, k	ku	firm, strong				
la, l	la	stay overnight				
yù, y	yù	eat, food				
ñ, r	ñ	pick				

As the script became a phonetic syllabary through successive revisions, the number of symbols was reduced from 466 in 1897 to 72 in 1918, and their forms became simpler. Njoya's phonetic achievements are praised, particularly his inclusion of a symbol for *glottal-stop*.

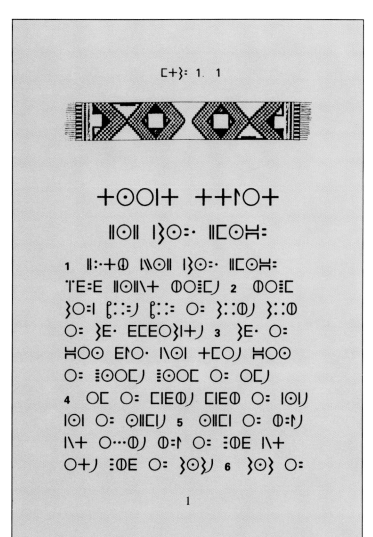

(*Above*) The Gospel of Matthew in the Tamajeq-Tuareg language of the Sahara, written in the Tifinagh alphabet. Published by SIM International, 1986.

(*Above right*) A page from a booklet entitled *The Story of the Children of Djimongu and Nfonte (The King of the Nte)* by King Njoya I, using the syllabary he developed for the Bamun language. Published in Cameroon, Africa, 1984.

(*Right*) Pages from the "test edition" of the Gospel of Luke in the Vai language. Two writing systems are used —the Vai syllabic (or Vai script) and the Vai Roman alphabet system. Published by the Institute of Liberian Languages, Liberia, Africa, 1984.

LÚKÌ 1

Sénjé-Kòàlì-Kùlè

ŏ lá mànjáă Tíófèló.

Mŏ kúlúŋ bà là à sùmà ànú ì kóĕ nú lŏ sèŋ à kè mú nú táyé là mú tĕ, ànú là à nyèl kílí mú mŏĕ nú là à fŏ ànú yè, à kè mú nú là kó bìlínú nú lŏ fèlè, à lá kùlù bí-bàndàă là, ămù ànú wá tŏŋ nì mŏ mú nú ànú là Kàmbàă-kò bìlínú nú lŏ sèŋ. 3 Kòmù wè mànjáă, ŏ pélé kílí mú wè, ŏ là kóĕ nú gbí lŏ kpèŋgbè, à ì bì à lá kùlù bí-bàndà mà, ŏ bè kùŋ lŏ kó tándé sá kpòló mà í lá kó là. 4 Ú bè kè má-nà bĕímáà ŏ wòló là í ì tóóbàă gbí sŏ kóĕ nú lŏ à kè mú nú ànú là í kàlà ànú là.

Wàtí mú ànú là JŏŋLá Wólé-WàndàĬ-Kùlè Wòŋ

5 Wàtí mú Hèlòdì tŏŋ mànjáă nú kùmà-mànjáă Jùdíà bóló ĕ lŏ, sálà bó àlìmáámì dòndó bè nì Àbìjà sálà bó àlìmáámlĕ nú tĕ kè mú tŏŋ nì Zàkèláyà. Ămù à là mùsúĕ tŏŋ nì Ìlésìbèl, à

PĀNINI,

famous grammarian
of the Sanskrit
language,

lived in India some time between the 7th c. and 4th c. B.C. Following in the steps of the Brahmi alphabet makers, he became the most renowned of the grammarians. His work on Sanskrit, with its 4,168 rules, is outstanding for its highly systematic methods of analyzing and describing language.

The phrases which illustrate his grammatical points are full of good humor:

"a dog old enough to lift a bone",
"occupying the whole chariot",
"an elephant-faced person", etc.

The birth of linguistic science in Western Europe in the 19th c. was due largely to the European discovery of Pānini's Sanskrit grammar, making linguistics a science.

The modern science of linguistics is the basis for producing alphabets for languages yet unwritten today.

Panini chats with farmers. He included their terminology and expressions in the language data on which he based his grammar.

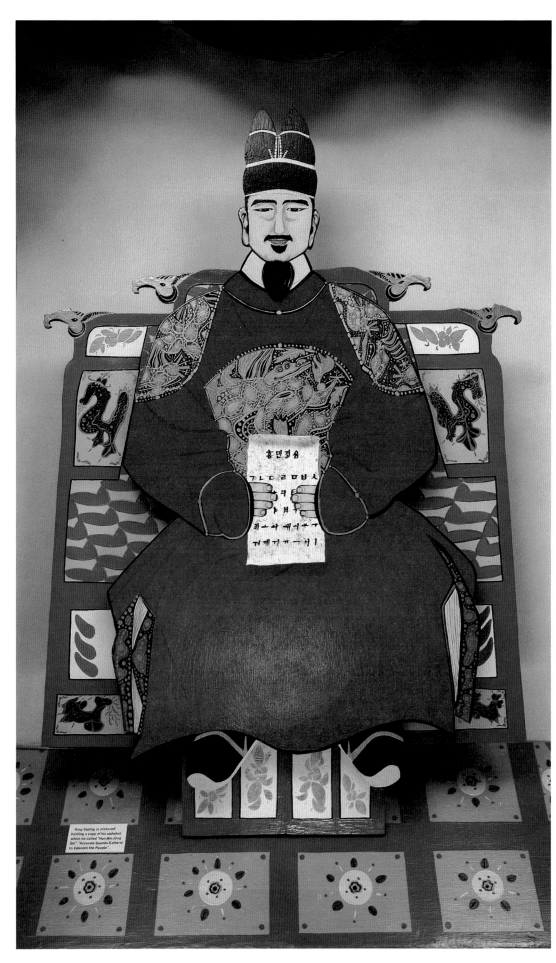

King Sejong is pictured holding a copy of his alphabet which he called "Hun Min Jong Ŭm", "Accurate Sounds (Letters) to Educate the People".

THE KOREAN ALPHABET
ONE OF THE WORLD'S MOST SCIENTIFIC

Though superficially similar to Chinese, which is not alphabetic, Korean is a true alphabet. It represents the individual sounds of the spoken language, and it does so in an unusually systematic way.

King Sejong (1397-1450) named his alphabet *Hun Min Jŏng Ŭm*, "Accurate Sounds to Educate the People," stating his purpose for creating it.

It is said that everywhere he went, the king took his portfolio of alphabet notes, and pursued this project that was closest to his heart.

Instead of using shapes descended from the North Semitic alphabet, as had much of the world, Sejong invented new shapes for letters.

The shapes reveal profound linguistic insights. Korea had been using Chinese characters, but few people could afford the years of study to learn that system. Sejong wanted an easy way to write Korean so that all could be literate.

It would also make printing with movable type far easier.

But the men of learning opposed Sejong's alphabet because it was not Chinese. They said it was too easy. Consequently, it was largely neglected, almost until the twentieth century. The use of the alphabet for a translation of the Bible helped popularize it.

Now called *Han'gŭl* in South Korea, and *Chosŏn Muntcha* in North Korea, it is the official alphabet in both countries.

The Korean alphabet has been called the most ingenious and scientific alphabet that is in general use in any country.

Sejong invented new shapes for letters, instead of using those descended from the North Semitic alphabet like the rest of the world.

The shapes themselves reveal profound linguistic insights.

CONSONANTS

Sejong described letters for 5 sets of consonant-sounds, each made by a different articulator in the mouth, saying that:

a) The basic letter of each set is a picture of the articulator for that set; and

b) Other letters of each set, built on the basic one by added strokes, represent speech-sounds made by the same articulator.

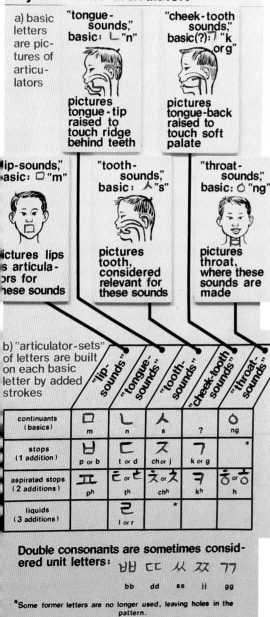

a) basic letters are pictures of articulators

"tongue-sounds," basic: ㄴ "n"
pictures tongue-tip raised to touch ridge behind teeth

"cheek-tooth sounds," basic (?): ㄱ "k or g"
pictures tongue-back raised to touch soft palate

"lip-sounds," basic: ㅁ "m"
pictures lips as articulators for these sounds

"tooth-sounds," basic: ㅅ "s"
pictures tooth, considered relevant for these sounds

"throat-sounds," basic: ㅇ "ng"
pictures throat, where these sounds are made

b) "articulator-sets" of letters are built on each basic letter by added strokes

	"lip-sounds"	"tongue-sounds"	"tooth-sounds"	"cheek-tooth sounds"	"throat-sounds"
continuants (basics)	ㅁ m	ㄴ n	ㅅ s	?	ㅇ ng
stops (1 addition)	ㅂ p or b	ㄷ t or d	ㅈ ch or j	ㄱ k or g	*
aspirated stops (2 additions)	ㅍ ph	ㅌ or ㅌ th	ㅊ or ㅊ chh	ㅋ kh	ㅎ or ㅎ h
liquids (3 additions)		ㄹ l or r		*	

Double consonants are sometimes considered unit letters: ㅃ ㄸ ㅆ ㅉ ㄲ
bb dd ss jj gg

*Some former letters are no longer used, leaving holes in the pattern.

VOWELS

There are 2 sets of vowels made at back and front tongue positions:
a) back has basic letters;
b) front has added stroke.

tongue backed   tongue fronted   ("palatalized")
(remember the 2 tongue-positions of Cyrillic vowels?)

Simple vowels

backed		fronted	
a (ah)	ㅏ	ㅑ	ya (yah)
ŏ (aw)	ㅓ	ㅕ	yŏ (yaw)
o	ㅗ	ㅛ	yo
u (oo)	ㅜ	ㅠ	yu (you)

2 simple vowels lack this contrast:
ㅣ (ee)   ㅡ (eu)

Diphthongs

backed		fronted	
e (eh)	ㅔ	ㅖ	ye (yeh)
ae	ㅐ	ㅒ	yae

Other diphthongs lack this contrast:
ㅢ (eui)   ㅘ (wa)
ㅚ oe   ㅙ oae (wae)   ㅟ ui (wi)   ㅝ uŏ (wŏ)   ㅞ ue (we)

In writing, letters are grouped by syllables into squares, to resemble Chinese characters.

Rules for grouping:
1) for consonant + vertical vowel, consonant is on left of vowel:
벼 byŏ "rice plant"   차 chha "car"   너 nŏ "you"

2) for consonant + horizontal vowel, consonant is above vowel:
코 kho "nose"   주 ju "Lord"   묘 myo "tomb"

3) for syllables with final consonants, these go below other letters:
삶 salm "life"   종 jong "bell"   집 jib "house"

4) for syllables beginning with a vowel, O is placed before vowel. (O is "ng" if ending a syllable, but silent before a vowel):
이 i "louse"   요 yo "Korean mat"   양 yang "sheep"

Notice grouping of letters in following words:
서울 Seoul   세종 Sejong

Some English sentences written in Korean letters:
How are you?   하우 아 유?
I go to school.   아이 고 투 스쿨
We had lunch.   위 해드 런치

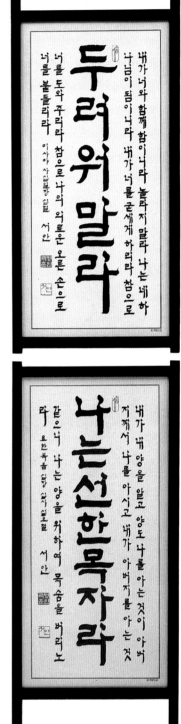

(*Above*) Examples of Korean alphabetical calligraphy for Biblical texts. The large script in the top one says, "Do not fear," with text of Isaiah 41:10 surrounding it. The large script in the bottom panel says, "I am the Good Shepherd," with text of John 10:14-15 surrounding it.

Pale ink is stronger than the most retentive mind.
—Confucius

CHINESE WRITING

Chinese is the oldest system in the world today, hardly changed in 4000 years. It is used by the world's largest nation—over a billion people.

Emperor Fu-Hsi (2852-2738 B.C.) was the legendary inventor of the Chinese script. His prewriting device, called the *Eight Trigrams*, was a combination of straight and broken lines apparently taken from marks on a turtle shell. This may have replaced knotted

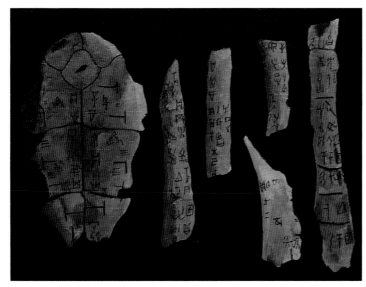

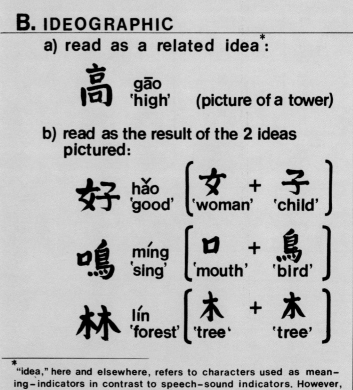

A. PICTOGRAPHIC
read as what it pictures*:

		origins	old	modern
rì	'sun'			日
shān	'hill'			山
zǐ	'child'			子
nǚ	'woman'			女
niǎo	'bird'			鳥
mù	'tree'			木
shuǐ	'water'			水 , 氵
mǎ	'horse'			馬
yáng	'sheep'			羊
tián	'field'			田

* "pictures," here and elsewhere, refer to the original forms, now hardly recognizable because of stylization.

B. IDEOGRAPHIC
a) read as a related idea*:

高 gāo 'high' (picture of a tower)

b) read as the result of the 2 ideas pictured:

好 hǎo 'good' [女 'woman' + 子 'child']

鳴 míng 'sing' [口 'mouth' + 鳥 'bird']

林 lín 'forest' [木 'tree' + 木 'tree']

* "idea," here and elsewhere, refers to characters used as meaning-indicators in contrast to speech-sound indicators. However, characters always represent definite words of spoken Chinese, not ideas that may be stated in different ways.

(*Above left*) Emperor Fu-Hsi and the Eight Trigrams (*see lower left corner*), said to be taken from marks on a turtle shell. (*Left*) Oracle bones.

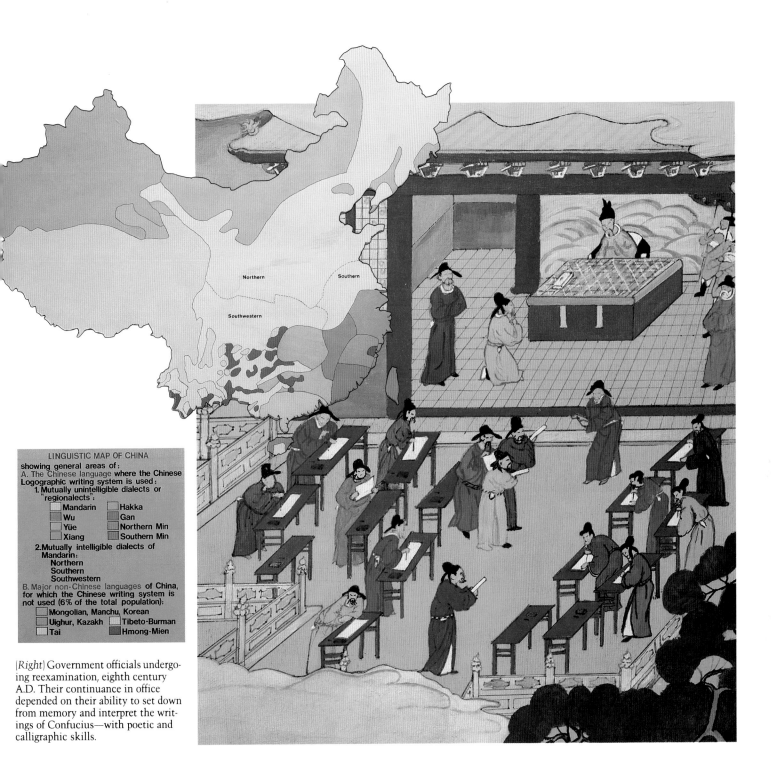

(*Right*) Government officials undergoing reexamination, eighth century A.D. Their continuance in office depended on their ability to set down from memory and interpret the writings of Confucius—with poetic and calligraphic skills.

cords which were used for record keeping.

About 2000 B.C., Chinese writing began as pictures. The earliest characters known (*about 1400 B.C.*) were on *oracle bones*. Some that were found still resembled the things they represented. But even then it was a full writing system, including representation of the spoken language.

There are reasons why the Chinese have not adopted an alphabet.

First: The difference between the dialects, or *regionalects*, is great. For instance, the word for *man* is pronounced *ren, yen, nene, nyin,* and *len* in different parts of China, but everywhere it is written 人. With an alphabet, Chinese would need to be written differently for each area. The single nonalphabetic writing system unites speakers of all Chinese dialects, and shows their common heritage.

Second: The language is loaded with *homophones*. Like *to, too,* and *two* in English, most Chinese words sound like several, or even dozens, of other words. Since alphabets represent words by their sounds only, it is hard to distinguish words that sound alike. But the Chinese system is ideally suited to handle homophones, as the writing distinguishes both meaning and sound. Moreover, most spoken and written words are paired with others, further distinguishing homophones.

Third: While an alphabet is ideal for writing words that have small changeable parts, like: *write, wrote, unwritten,* and *writer's,* Chinese words do not have changeable parts. The grammar works by adding and rearranging whole words, rather than parts.

Therefore, the *logographic* system, with unchanging symbols for whole words, fits Chinese well.

For the Chinese, calligraphy serves as a display of a person's moral and spiritual worth. In 3000 years, different materials and uses have created a variety of styles. The following are for the word fish (yú):

Seal script, drawn or engraved on bone, cast in bronze, stamped in clay, etc.

Standard brush script, used since the fourth century, is the regular script of today.

Running script, a cursive style for fast writing.

Grass script, a shorthand style allowing for personal expression.

Writing has traditionally been from top to bottom, the columns proceeding from right to left. But in China today the favored direction is horizontal, from left to right.

大風起兮雲飛揚、威加海
內兮歸故鄉安得猛士兮
守四方

漢高祖
大風歌
乙丑年歲在辰戌夏日森耀書

天淨沙一首
馬致遠
辰戌夏日森耀方於海之

CALLIGRAPHIC BRUSHSTROKES

Brushstrokes are the basic units of which the calligraphic characters are constructed. Traditionally eight in number, they form a standard set. The strokes are exemplified by the character for *yǔng* (forever):

永 (strokes numbered 1–8)

The number of strokes, like alphabetical order, is the basis for arranging Chinese characters. Dictionaries arrange the symbols according to the number of strokes of the *radicals*, then of the remainder of each character.

2 strokes:	12 strokes:	23 strokes
几	跑	響
chī (bench)	*paǒ* (to run)	*xiǎng* (echo)

No matter how many strokes, each character fits an invisible square.

WRITING REFORMS

Simplification has reduced the number of strokes for over 2000 most frequently used characters. In most cases, this meant giving official status to forms used informally:

马 for 馬 *mǎ* (horse)
电 for 電 *diàn* (electricity)
坏 for 壞 *huài* (bad)

The number of strokes per character now averages about the same as letters per English word. This reform has greatly fostered literacy. Everything published in the People's Republic of China since 1956 has been in the simplified characters. Other Chinese use the old forms.

Pīnyīn, Chinese written with the Roman alphabet, was made the official phonetic alphabet for the People's Republic of China. It has several uses but is not considered a replacement for characters.

The calligraphy is from two different pieces of Chinese literature, (*left*) in grass style and (*above*) in standard style. Smaller writing identifies the author, his title, the date, and gives a melody for singing. The *red chops* authenticate the calligrapher.

JAPANESE WRITING
"CHINESE, PLUS"

Like other countries on Asia's outer edge, Japan was influenced by China. The Chinese writing system was relayed to Japan by Korea in the fourth century A.D.

Calligraphy is as important to the Japanese as to the Chinese. The most admired, for both official and everyday use, is the hard-to-read grass style.

As with Chinese, Japanese is read from top to bottom, beginning on the right, or horizontally, from left to right.

Though Chinese culture and masses of Chinese words and characters were assimilated by the Japanese, it was

some time before Japanese could be written, for Chinese writing was not easily adaptable to Japanese, a language of an entirely different kind.

Only in the matter of word roots was it similar, for example:

means "mountain" (pronounced *shān* in Chinese and *yama* in Japanese);

花

means "flower" (*huā* in Chinese and *hana* in Japanese).

However, Japanese could not function without its

many grammatical parts, for which there were no Chinese characters. Something had to be added to Chinese characters in order to write Japanese.

The Japanese developed a system which uses *unmodified* Chinese characters, chosen for their Chinese *meanings*, called *kanji*, to write Japanese word roots; and *abbreviated* Chinese characters, chosen for their Chinese *sounds*, called *kana*, to write everything else. The two are normally used together.

Kana consists of two different sets of 50 characters each. Since each kana character represents a syllable of speech rather than a single sound, the two sets are called syllabaries, not alphabets. These two syllabaries are called *hiragana* and *katakana*.

Hiragana characters are simplified forms of *cursive* Chinese characters, used to write such parts of Japanese as suffixes and prepositions. Katakana characters are simplified forms of *standard* Chinese characters used mainly to write borrowed Western words.

Although their spoken language has only 112 different syllables (English has about 3000), theirs is the most complex of today's major writing systems.

THE TRADITIONAL INVENTOR OF HIRAGANA

Kūkai, or Kobo Daishi, a Buddhist abbot (774-835), is thought to have played a major role in standardizing hiragana. The process continued until the late nineteenth century.

The first writers of Japanese had used whole Chinese characters for meaning and sound with no indication of which way it was to be read.

Standardization of hiragana entailed (1) analyzing Japanese speech to determine what the syllables were; (2) choosing from among the

many possibilities one Chinese character to represent each syllable of spoken Japanese; (3) modifying these characters so that a reader could distinguish them from kanji at a glance.

Kūkai wanted all people to learn to read and write. He started a school for commoners' children. Though it was not continued after his death, the value of literacy had become an entrenched idea, and today the Japanese are among the best educated and literate people in the world.

LADIES OF LETTERS

Women of the Japanese aristocracy in the ninth to eleventh centuries A.D. were among the first to benefit from hiragana, the Japanese syllabary. It enabled them to produce some fine literature, including the world's first great novel, *Tale of Genji*, by Lady Murasaki Shikibu. Meanwhile, the men continued to struggle with Chinese characters, considered too difficult for women.

In words pressed onto paper lie man's best hopes of doing something more than merely surviving.

—John Hersey

LITERACY-ADVANCING IDEAS OF EAST ASIA

THE DEVELOPMENT OF PAPER AND PRINTING

In A.D. 105 Ts'ài Lun of China invented paper, making it of tree bark, hemp, rags, and fishnets.

Before that time papyrus, parchment, and vellum had been used for writing in the West. In the East, silk, wood, and bamboo had been used.

However, Ts'ài Lun's invention did not cross the borders of China for more than 600 years. So these other substances continued to be used for centuries.

In A.D. 751 Arabs captured some Chinese papermakers

who taught them their trade. The Arabs set up the first paper factory outside China at Samarkand, located in what is now the U.S.S.R.

The art spread westward to Baghdad (A.D. 793), Damascus, Egypt (A.D. 900), Morocco (A.D. 1100), and Spain (A.D. 1150). Europeans were introduced to paper when it was brought to Spain, over 1000 years after its invention.

Papermaking today is basically the same as it was in Ts'ài Lun's time.

From early times, the Chinese made rubbings from inked stone inscriptions and impressions from inked seals or stamps.

The transition to larger blocks in the seventh or eighth century A.D. marks the beginning of block printing.

The earliest block prints now in existence are Buddhist charms, made in Japan in A.D. 770. The world's oldest known printed book, *The Diamond Sutra*, was block printed in China in A.D. 868 by Wang Kie, the first printer whose name we know.

In A.D. 1045, Pì Shēng invented movable type. Chinese movable type was first made from clay and later from wood and metal. But the thousands of characters in Chinese made the invention an impractical one for printers. They found it easier to continue to use block printing, in which a whole page of text was carved into a block of wood.

Metal type cast in molds was first used about A.D. 1400 in Korea.

There is not enough evidence to link the invention of movable type in China and Korea with the discoveries in Europe that led to the development of the printing press there.

(*Left*) Dipping the mold in the vat of water and pulp, and setting the sheets out to dry—paper making today follows the basic principles of its first invention in China.
(*Above*) Carved woodblock for printing a page of Korean in Chinese characters. Note that characters are reversed.
(*Right*) "The paper route" from China to Europe, which took over 1000 years.

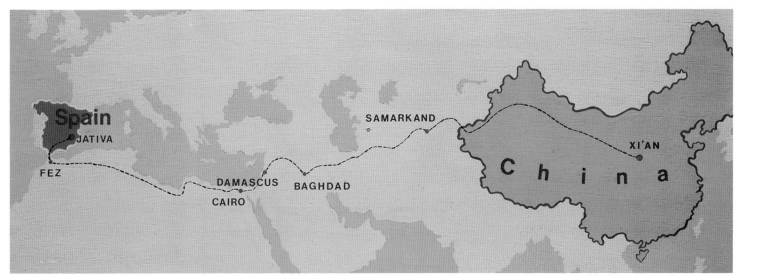

NORTH AMERICAN SCRIPTS

CREE SYLLABLE-ALPHABET
A UNIQUE INVENTION

While the Cree Indians sit out the long winter evenings waiting on their trap lines, they read. Every week, with the help of computers, new reading material is produced in Cree. The literature is written in their unusual "alphabet," originally created for the translation of the Bible.

This unique alphabet has passed from the Cree to the Ojibwa (speakers of a similar Algonquian language), to the Chipewyan, Beaver, and Slavey (members of the Athapascan language family), and finally to the Eastern Arctic Eskimo.

Compare the length of *"I wish he had killed that caribou,"* in Cree, using Evans's symbols:

ᑲᒫ ᒋ-ᓂᐸᐦᐊᑯᐸᓀ ᐊᓂᔪᐤ ᐊᑎᒄ·ᑲ

and in the Roman alphabet:

Kamaa chii-nipahaakupane aniyuu atihkwa.

LUKE 8
(page 202)

Ciisahs ekiiwiintank kaaicikaatenik aawehcikewin kihtikaanenhsan ehtashincikaatekin

(Matthew 13.18-23; Mark 4.13-20)

11 "Mii ohsha ohowe aawehcikewin eihkitoomakahk; kihtikaanenhsan ohsha mii howe otihkitowin Kishemanitoo. 12Kihtikaanenhsan kaakiihpankihsinkin kaaishipimamonk miihkana, oncikihkinawaacinaakwan ahaweniwak kaakiinoontaminit, piko tahsh macimanitoo piishaa miina eotaahpinamawaat ohowe kihkinohamaakewin kaakiihpinaakatawentamowaat. Mii hiwe wenci-ishihciket ekaa citepwehtaminit miina ekaa cipîmaacihikoowisinit. 13Kihtikaanenhsan kaakiihpankihsinkin kaaishiahsiniiwahkamikaak, oncikihkinawaacinaakwan ahaweniwak kaakiinoontamowaat Kishemanitoo otihkitowin, miina ekiiotaahpinamowaat minwaatamowinink. Piko tahsh ishinaakosiwak kihtikaanenhs ekaa kaawatapiiwank. Tepwehtamowak hsa wiin acina piko. Ahpii eishiihsek ehkocihikoowisiwaat, mii himaa eishinoontepoonihcikewaat. 14Ekwa tahsh kihtikaanenhsan kaakiihpankihsinkin mekweyahii okaawiminakashiihkaank, oncikihkinawaacinaakwan ahaweniwak kaakiinoontamowaat, piko tahsh mikoshkaatentamowin miina wenootisiwin kaye minwentamowaatisiwin emooshkineshkaakowaat ohomaa pimaatisiwinink, okipishkaakonaawaa. Mii hiwe ishinaakosiwak kihtikaanenhsink kaakiiani-ishinipoomakahkin miina omiinihshiwiniwaa ekaa ekiioncikiishinihtaawikininik. 15Kihtikaanenhsan tahsh kaakiihpankihsinkin kaaishiminwahkamikaak, oncikihkinawaacinaakwan ahaweniwak kaakiinoontamowaat Kishemanitoo otihkitowin miina eminokanawentamowaat miina enanahihtamowaat otehiwaank, miina eaayiicimincinimamowaat, mii tahsh ohomaa oshiipentamowiniwaank wencianiminomiinihshiwiwaat.

Eaawehcikaaket waahsahkonencikan

(Mark 4.21-25)

16"Awiya sahkahank waahsahkonencikanini kaawin otaa-akwanahansiin mihtikowashini ciaapacihtoot. Kaawin kaye shekonipewin otaa-ahtoohsiin. Ekwa tahsh nawac waahsahkonencikanaahtikonk otahtoon, ihiwe onci anihshininiwak ciwaapantamowaat ewaahsahkonenik ahpii ehpiintikewaat.

17"Piko tahsh kekoon kaakaacikaatek tapiicikaate kaaishiwaahseyaak, miina piko kekoon kaa-aakawahikaatek tamihkikaate miina cipiicikaatek kaaishiwaahseyaak.

Mr. Evans's invention of the Cree syllabic characters was an act of genius.
—Bruce Peel

In the Cree writing system one symbol is used for each syllable. Their 12 letters represent 48 syllables. The direction the consonants face indicates which vowel is being used.

James Evans, a missionary who went to Canada to live with the Cree in 1840, was the inventor of their writing system.

Needing a way to write their language for Bible translation, he first tried using the Roman alphabet. However, the sounds of Cree were so different from English that his attempts at translation confused the Cree readers. So Evans invented his own letters. Cree words tend to be long. To shorten their written forms, Evans used one letter for each syllable, plus some small distinguishing marks.

The letters rotate in 4 directions to indicate the four vowels:

For Type A letters,
"up"=-i, "down"=-e,
"left"=-a, "right"=-u.

For Type B letters,
"up and right"=-i,
"up and left"=-e,
"down and right"=-a,
"down and left"=-u.

The basic shape of the letter (wedge, fish-hook, arch, etc.) represents the consonant:

ᐱ=pi ᐯ=pe ᐸ=pa ᐳ=pu
ᓯ=si ᓭ=se ᓴ=sa ᓱ=su

One basic shape, a triangle, represents a vowel when used as a syllable in itself:

ᐃ=i ᐁ=e ᐊ=a ᐅ=u

Syllable-final consonants are indicated by the letter facing in the direction for "a", but smaller and raised:

ᐸᒼ=pam ᑫᓪ=kel ᐊᑦ=at

Type A letters

phonetic values	↑=-i as in it	↓=-e as in end	←=-a as in far	→=-u as in up	syllable-final consonants
p-	ᐱ	ᐯ	ᐸ	ᐳ	ᑉ
r-	ᕆ	ᕂ	ᕋ	ᕈ	ᕐ
t-	ᑎ	ᑌ	ᑕ	ᑐ	ᑦ
vowel as syllable	ᐃ	ᐁ	ᐊ	ᐅ	-h ᐦ

Type B letters

	↱=-i	↰=-e	↳=-a	↲=-u	
ch-	ᒋ	ᒉ	ᒐ	ᒍ	ᒡ
k-	ᑭ	ᑫ	ᑲ	ᑯ	ᒃ
l-	ᓕ	ᓓ	ᓚ	ᓗ	ᓪ
m-	ᒥ	ᒣ	ᒪ	ᒧ	ᒼ
n-	ᓂ	ᓀ	ᓇ	ᓄ	ᓐ
s-	ᓯ	ᓭ	ᓴ	ᓱ	ᔅ
sh-	ᔑ	ᔐ	ᔕ	ᔓ	ᔥ
y-	ᔨ	ᔦ	ᔭ	ᔪ	ᔾ

A double vowel is indicated by a dot above the letter:

ᐹ=paa ᒎ=chuu

A "w" between the consonant and vowel is indicated by a dot before the letter:

·ᐸ=pwa ·ᑫᓪ=kwel

The Cree found their new writing system easy to learn. It is said a man could learn to read in half a day. Trappers helped spread the alphabet across most of the width of Canada until nearly every Cree learned to read.

In order to print material for the new readers, Evans converted a fur-pressing machine into a printing press. He used inner layers of birch bark for paper. His ink was soot mixed with fish oil. He made movable type from the lead lining of tea chests. Deerskin covered his books.

Evans surrounded himself with Cree helpers who did the major portion of the translation work. One of these, Thomas Hassel, Evans accidentally shot and killed while passing a loaded gun in a canoe. He was advised to flee, to escape being killed in revenge. Instead, Evans turned himself in to the grieving parents, who adopted him as their son. He later cared for them in their old age.

A literate man feels master of his fate.
— Mary Burnet

THE CHEROKEE SYLLABARY
AN UNEQUALED ACCOMPLISHMENT

Cherokee is an Iroquoian Indian language spoken today by about 12,000 people in Oklahoma and North Carolina. Originally from the southeastern United States, the Cherokee were removed to Oklahoma in the 1830s.

Sequoyah (c. 1765-1843) is one of the great names in American history. Sequoyah, though illiterate, created a writing system, a task undertaken in modern times only by highly trained linguists. His creation made his nation literate in a few months.

Convinced that the white man's power lay in his written language, he determined to provide the same for Cherokee. After 12 years of hard work he had completed his set of 85 symbols representing all the sounds of his language.

To name the letters, one by one, was to read the word, as if (in English) *"enemy"* were written *"n-m-e,"* and *"Elsie," "L-c."*

But he had to convince the tribal elders that it worked. So he and his ten-year-old daughter Ah-yoka, whom he had taught to read and write, carried out a demonstration. Sequoyah left the house while Ah-yoka wrote what the skeptical elders dictated. When he returned, he read all that she had written.

The elders were dumbfounded, then ecstatic. Their own language could be written. It was as good as English.

Literacy caught on like wildfire. Soon these woodland hunters were more literate in two languages than the white population was in one. A steady stream of literature poured from their own press, in Cherokee and English.

(*Right*) Sequoyah, reading a message written by his ten-year-old daughter, Ah-yoka, using the syllabic script he devised for writing Cherokee.

The Cherokee Syllabary, with Phonetic Values

	a	e	i	o	u	ʌ
	D (a)	**R** (e)	**T** (i)	**Ꮒ** (o)	**O'** (u)	**i** (ʌ)
ka / ga	**Ꭶ** (ka)	**F** (ga)	**Ᏺ** (ge)	**У** (gi)	**A** (go)	**J** (gu) · **E** (gʌ)
ha		**?** (he)	**Ꭿ** (hi)	**Ᏻ** (ho)	**Γ** (hu)	**Ꮜ** (hʌ) · **Ꮀ** (ha)
la	**W** (la)	**♂** (le)	**ſ** (li)	**Ꮑ** (lo)	**M** (lu)	**Ꮑ** (lʌ)
ma	**ᏸ** (ma)	**Ol** (me)	**H** (mi)	**Ꮂ** (mo)	**y** (mu)	
hna nah / na	**Ꮏ** (hna) **G** (nah) **θ** (na)	**Ʌ** (ne)	**h** (ni)	**Z** (no)	**ꟼ** (nu)	**Oʻ** (nʌ)
kwa	**Ᏺ** (kwa)	**Ꮽ** (kwe)	**P** (kwi)	**Ꮺ** (kwo)	**Ꮽ** (kwu)	**Ɛ** (kwʌ)
s / sa	**Ꮝ** (s) **Ʊ** (sa)	**4** (se)	**b** (si)	**Ᏺ** (so)	**ℰ** (su)	**R** (sʌ)
da	**Ꮧ** (da)	**Ꮥ** (de)	**Ꮧ** (di)	**V** (do)	**S** (du)	**σ** (dʌ)
ta	**W** (ta)	**Ꮷ** (te)	**Ꮧ** (ti)			
dla / tla	**Ꮫ** (dla) **Ꮣ** (tla)	**L** (tle)	**C** (tli)	**Ꮵ** (tlo)	**Ꮲ** (tlu)	**P** (tlʌ)
tsa	**G** (tsa)	**V** (tse)	**Ir** (tsi)	**K** (tso)	**J** (tsu)	**C** (tsʌ)
wa	**Ꮤ** (wa)	**Ꮻ** (we)	**θ** (wi)	**Ꮼ** (wo)	**Ꮽ** (wu)	**6** (wʌ)
ya	**Ꮿ** (ya)	**β** (ye)	**Ꭹ** (yi)	**ꮀ** (yo)	**Gʻ** (yu)	**B** (yʌ)

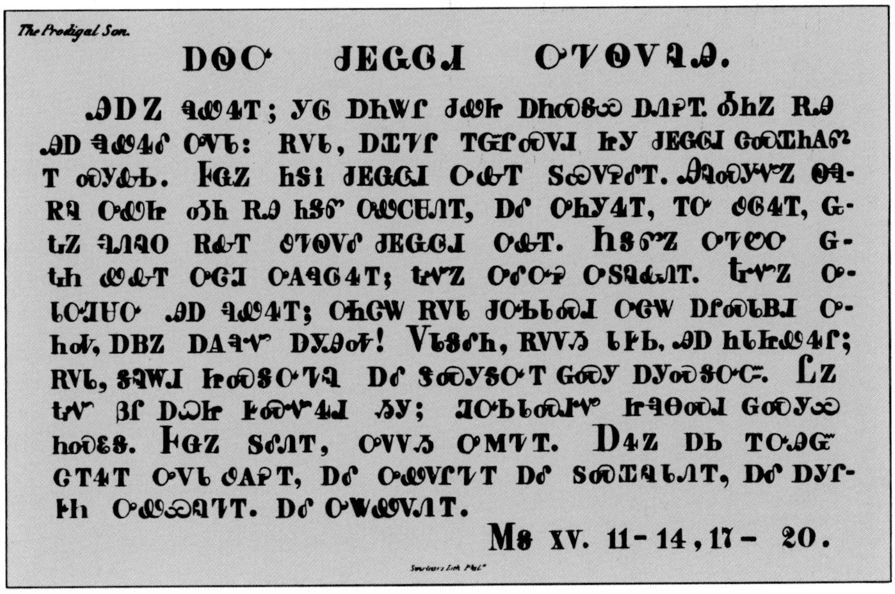

How does one write his language? By making a picture of each one of its thousands of words?

🏔 = snow,   🌵 = desert,

◈ = wisdom,   ⌣ = chief.

This is how Sequoyah started to invent a writing system for his own Cherokee language. He drew his symbols with pokeberry juice on chips of wood. But the number of them grew hopelessly large.

When his wife, angered over his neglect of the family, threw his entire cache of chips into the fire, Sequoyah started on a new track.

He noticed that just a few recurrent sounds of speech combined to form numerous words. He listened as Cherokees talked. After many years he was satisfied he had discovered all the different syllables that made up his language—just 85.

To symbolize these, he did not use pictures, but took some letters of the English alphabet, changed some, invented others, until he had enough. But, not being a reader of English, he didn't know the sound values of the letters, so he did his own assigning of letter to sound.

Each letter stands for a whole syllable, which makes this a syllabary, not an alphabet.

Thus we find: H=*mi*, Z=*no*, D=*a*, b=*si*, etc.

The three letters ᏣᎳᎩ spell *Tsa-la-gi*, the Cherokee form of the tribe's name, and the letters ᏍᏉᏯ spell Sequoyah's name phonetically: *Si-kwo-ya*.

The presence of one alphabet letter (a symbol for a single speech sound rather than a syllable), Ꮝ for *s*, combines with many other consonants: *sdi*, *sga*, etc., and shortens the syllabary considerably.

The Prodigal Son.

ᎠᏂ ᏕᎦᏅᎩ ᎤᏤᎷᏨᏍ.

[Cherokee syllabary text — The Prodigal Son]

Mɛ XV. 11-14, 17-20.

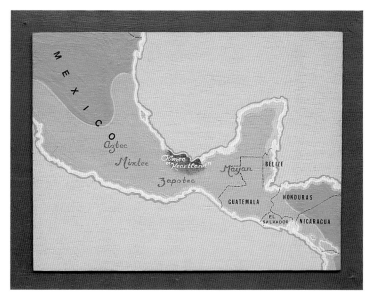

MESOAMERICAN SCRIPTS

In the tropical Gulf Coast of Mexico, the Olmecs founded the only civilization with writing in the pre-Columbian Americas.

Between 1200 and 400 B.C. they spread their culture complex, which the Maya later developed to a remarkable degree. It included astronomy, mathematics, and the beginning of writing.

The Olmec sphere defines the cultural area known as Mesoamerica (Middle America).

MAYAN NUMBERS

A true place value number writing system was invented, in about 600 B.C., probably by the Olmecs. A replica of "Stela C" from Tres Zapotes, Veracruz, Mexico (*above right*), carries one of the earliest dates found in the Americas: 7.16.6.16.18. In the European dating system it would be 31 B.C.

THE MAYAN CALENDAR

The Maya perfected the Mesoamerican method of calculating dates. Generations of astronomer-priests built up an amazing store of knowledge. It was of utmost importance to them to figure combinations of astronomical cycles so they could harmonize their own activities with the heavens. Their calendar was as accurate as the one used today.

MAYAN WRITING

The Maya developed Mesoamerican writing to its highest form. Apparently they could write anything they could say.

The reproduction of a jade pectoral (*above*), about 50 B.C., is the oldest readable Mayan text known, and seems to be transitional between Olmec and Maya.

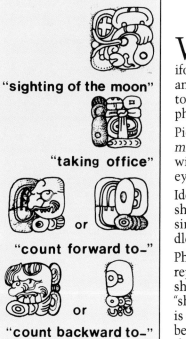

"sighting of the moon"

"taking office"

or

"count forward to–"

or

"count backward to–"

Writing was of the combination type, like cuneiform, Egyptian hieroglyphics and Chinese, combining pictograms, ideograms, and phonograms.

Pictograms—*Sighting of the moon* is shown by a head with lines coming from the eye to a small moon.

Ideograms—*Taking office* is shown by a tied-up bundle, since a ruler received a bundle on accession to office.

Phonograms—*To count* is represented by the head of a shark; both "count" and "shark" are pronounced *xoc*. It is also represented by a jade bead, an ideogram for "water," the environment of the shark.

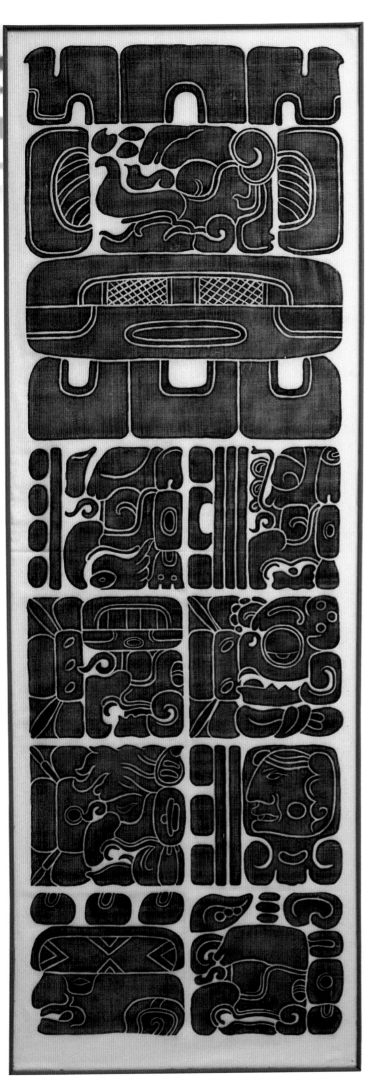

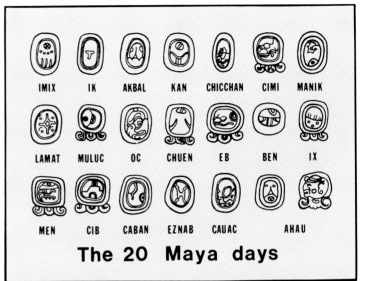

The 20 Maya days

IMIX · IK · AKBAL · KAN · CHICCHAN · CIMI · MANIK

LAMAT · MULUC · OC · CHUEN · EB · BEN · IX

MEN · CIB · CABAN · EZNAB · CAUAC · AHAU

(*Above*) A replica of a Zapotec Indian pottery figure, called "The Scribe of Cuilapan," Monte Albán II, 200 B.C.–A.D. 100. The glyph on the hat means "13 water," that on the chest, "13-flint-knife." One of the two is probably the man's calendar name.

(*Above and below*) Calendrical day signs, from Palenque, Mexico.

Introductory glyph with patron deity of month on which date falls: "Cumkú"		= 9 baktuns or 1,296,000 days
Date in time-periods		=17 katuns or 122,400 days
		= 0 tuns or 0 days
		= 0 uinals or 0 days
Day on which this date falls: "13 Ahau"		= 0 kins or 0 days
Information about the moon		Total = 1,418,400 days since their starting date, like European calendars — start with the birth of Christ

(*Left*) Cloth rubbing showing "Initial Series," Long count date, from Maya Stela E, east side; Quiriguá, Guatemala; celebrating end of Katun 17 (A.D. 771).

There is something insulting about teaching a man a series of separate skills without teaching him how to learn more.

—Mary Burnet

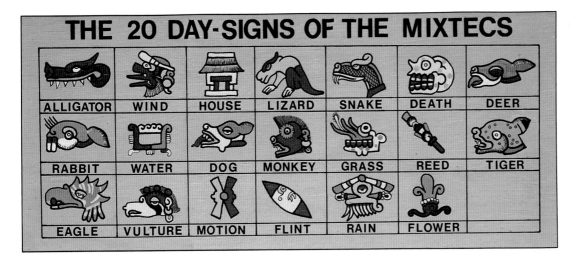

THE 20 DAY-SIGNS OF THE MIXTECS

ALLIGATOR	WIND	HOUSE	LIZARD	SNAKE	DEATH	DEER
RABBIT	WATER	DOG	MONKEY	GRASS	REED	TIGER
EAGLE	VULTURE	MOTION	FLINT	RAIN	FLOWER	

(*Above*) Part of a Mixtec pictogram showing One-Vulture having peaceful dealings with the Spaniards.

(*Top*) As in the European system, names of days accompanied numbers to give a full date. Day signs were used for writing dates, place-names, and personal "calendar" names.

(*Above*) An example of Mixtec writing, a record of a covenant between two rulers. Translated, it reads, "At Ballcourt Hill—year: two-arrow, day: four-eagle—Princess Two-Vulture and Prince Seven-Motion, made an agreement."

MIXTEC-AZTEC SCRIPT

The Mixtec Indians of Mexico, influenced by the Zapotecs, developed their own script by A.D. 900. Mixtec writing was less advanced than that of the Maya, who used *phonograms* (symbols representing sounds) throughout their writing. In contrast, the Mixtec used them only in writing names.

The Mixtec calendar was based on a 52-year cycle. They did not number years beyond 52.

About A.D. 1400 the Aztecs adopted Mixtec ways of writing except for the year symbol and calendar names of persons.

Following the Spanish conquest (A.D. 1521), place-name writing developed into a phonemic syllabary before being discontinued.

Their non-calendrical number symbols, except for dots, are probably original: 1-19, dots or one or two fingers; 20, flag; 400, hair or tree; 8000, bag of copal balls.

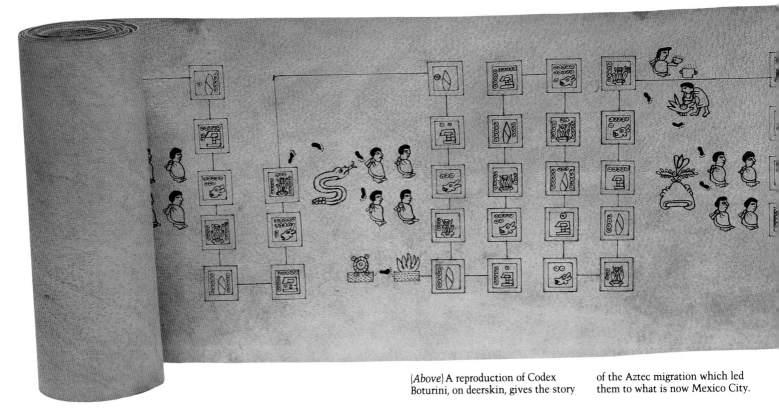

(*Above*) A reproduction of Codex Boturini, on deerskin, gives the story of the Aztec migration which led them to what is now Mexico City.

RECORD-KEEPING OF THE INCAS

The Incas of Peru, rulers of a vast empire, were without writing. But they had an efficient device for recording statistics: the *quipu*, "knots." It used a decimal place-value system. Each level of knots, moving upward, represented one higher power of 10.

The different colors and grouping of the strings gave it multi-dimensional capabilities.

The Incas obtained and maintained political cohesiveness by forced resettlement of the over 100 ethnic groups they conquered, spreading them throughout the empire. They ruled 12 million people who spoke many different languages.

The first grammar and lexicon of the Quechua language was published in 1595 after the Spanish conquest in 1532. However, Quechua is really the name for a group of related languages. Today, there are about 45 Quechuan languages spoken in South America. Through the work of SIL and mission organizations, many of these descendants of the Incas now have an alphabet for their language. Some have the New Testament and other literature as well.

Can you count in knots?

As early as the end of the 4th millennium B.C. proto-Sumerian and proto-Elamite scribes had well-developed systems of numbers and measures.
—Joran Friberg

THE WRITING OF NUMBERS

Some authorities hold that the origin of writing was motivated by religion; others, by a need to remember dates for planting crops. Still others believe that economics created the need. Whichever it was, or whether it was a combination of these reasons, a system for keeping inventories and recording business dealings was certainly an early necessity. In the earliest times, numbers were recorded with three-dimensional tokens (see chart *right*).

Today the meaning of numbers depends on the order in which they're written. For example, in many countries of the world, people recognize the number 312 as being different from the number 213. However, the way people interpret groups of numbers has varied—and continues to vary—from one culture to another.

Some people have used an *additive* numeration system, in which numbers are repeated to produce a total. In this system, 111 would represent the number three.

In the *multiplicative* numeration system, pairs of numbers are multiplied and their products added to obtain the value of the number being written. For example, the number 16 could be represented by 2721 (two times seven plus two times one).

The most widely used system today is the *place value* system, in which the place each number occupies indicates its value, or *power*. For example, 312 represents three hundreds, one ten and two ones. The value of the number is the sum of the three numbers after each has been multiplied by its power.

Modern industry and science rely on the place value system, passed on to Europe from India and Arabia. Many other cultures have either adopted the system or adapted it.

	TOKENS	ARCHA-IC from 3200 B.C.	CUNEI-FORM from 2700 B.C.
1			
10			
60			
600 (60 x 10)			
3,600 (60^2)			
36,000 (60^2 x 10)			
216,000 (60^3)	?	?	

(*Top*) Originating in Sumeria about 3200 B.C., the earliest known numbering system was derived from clay tokens (*left column*). The archaic and cuneiform systems (*middle* and *right* columns) had symbols for *1, 10,* and *60* and its multiples. The symbols were added to find the value of the number being represented, making it an additive numeration system.

(*Above*) A replica of a clay tablet from Uruk in Sumer containing one of the earliest examples of writing. The writer held the stylus at an angle to the clay for D-shaped impressions and perpendicular to it for circular ones.

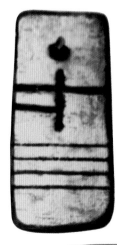

The numbers scribed on the replicas of the Etruscan wooden sticks (*above*) are: top, 19; middle, 190; and bottom, 257.

(*Below*) The Greek treasurer is using pebbles on a counting board (abacus). Columns are marked with numerals of the acrophonic system. Each numeral is the first letter of the number-word: **M** = murioi, *ten thousand*; **Ψ** (or **X**) = Khilioi, *thousand*; **H** = hekaton, *hundred*; **▷** = deka, *ten*; **Γ** = pente, *five*; **O** symbolizes *one*; the rest are fractions. From a fourth century B.C. vase.

(*Above*) A model of a simple Roman abacus shows how the place value system was derived from the arrangement of counters on the instrument.

THE ABACUS

The place value system developed from the use of the abacus for mathematics. An early abacus was the ancient Greek *abax*, a table or board on which columns of pebbles were lined up as counters. Throughout history, it has had many different forms.

This is how an abacus works. A counter, placed on the first line on the right of the abacus, is valued at one. Each counter on the line to the left is worth 10 of the ones, and each one on the next line is worth 10 of the 10's, or 100. (A place value system in which the power of each number in a sequence increases by a multiple of 10 has a *decimal base*.)

Because the place where the counters were located gave them their value, they had "place value." The lines of the abacus have disappeared, but the placement of a number still signifies its power.

INDO-ARABIC SYSTEM

Europe inherited its numbering system from India via Arabia. From the fifth century A.D., Indians used a place value numbering system, possibly derived directly from the abacus or modified from the way the Babylonians or Chinese wrote numbers. Chinese used "rod numerals," numbers written across an abacus-like grid, with each empty space representing zero.

Filling the empty spaces with zero results in a numbering system similar, in principle, to the one used today.

The Indian system, introduced to Islamic countries in the eighth century A.D., was in use by the Arabs in Spain by the ninth century. From there, it spread throughout Europe and replaced the abacus by the fifteenth century.

(*Right*) By adopting India's place value system, the Arabs were enabled to contribute to the fields of algebra and trigonometry.

SPECIAL TYPES OF COMMUNICATION
THE WRITING OF MUSIC

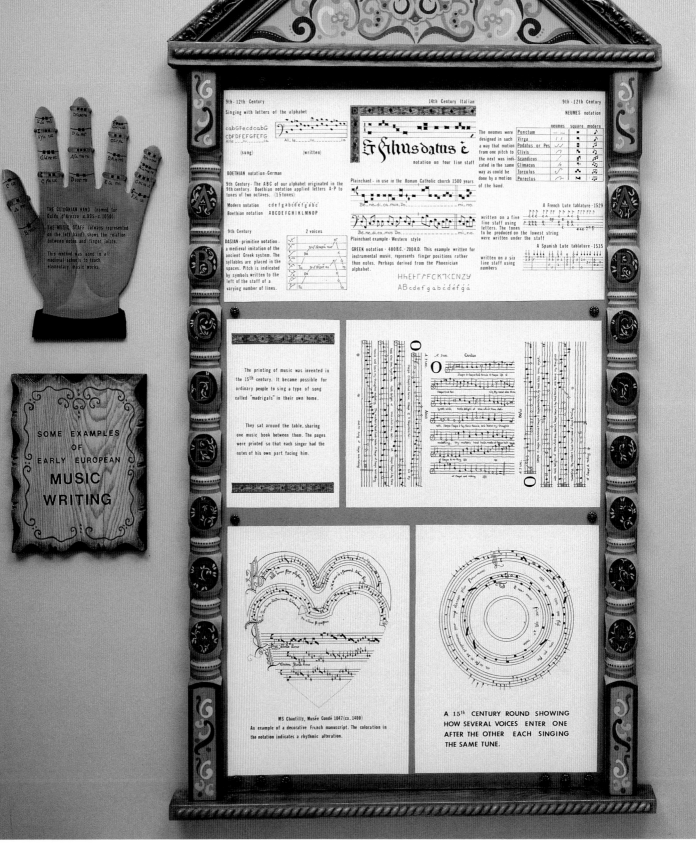

THE SONG TABLET OF UGARIT

3 AN ASSYRIAN SONG CATALOGUE

1 OLD BABYLONIAN AKKADIAN MATHEMATICAL TEXT GIVES US NAMES OF LYRE STRINGS—INTERVALS BETWEEN STRINGS

FOUR CUNEIFORM TABLETS FROM DIFFERENT PARTS OF MESOPOTAMIA PROVIDED THE KEY FOR UNDER—STANDING THE NOTATION SYSTEM OF THE SONG TABLET. THE SONG TABLET WAS FOUND IN UGARIT.

UGARIT

ASSUR

NIPPUR

UR

4 OLD BABYLONIAN AKKADIAN TEXT INSTRUCTIONS FOR TUNING A LYRE

2 SUMERIAN-AKKADIAN LEXICAL TEXT DEALING WITH MUSICAL TERMS

The earliest-known musical notation was written in cuneiform on a clay tablet circa 1400 B.C. The Hurrian song (below the double line) is to be played in the *Nid-qabli* tuning, which is the same as the major "do, re, mi" scale. The notes indicate both the melody (upper note) and accompaniment (lower note).

This tablet was excavated at the ancient city of Ugarit (modern Ras Shamra) on the Syrian coast. It is one complete cult hymn. The lyric is written in the now dead Hurrian language. Even though imperfectly understood, one phrase is clear: "Thou, the goddess, lovest them in thy heart."

It was previously thought that two-part harmony appeared no earlier than the European Middle Ages. Hurrian music does not have indications for rhythm, tempo, or musical ornamentation. The text above the double line is the lyric of the song.

The lyre model is a typical *bull lyre* common to the third millennium in Mesopotamia. It was one of several stringed instruments found in the royal tomb at Ur in 1927. The eight to thirteen strings were tuned by adjusting the pegs on the crossbar.

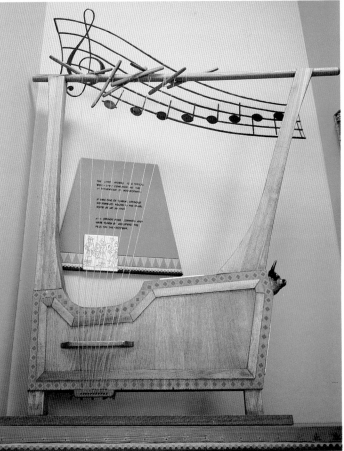

SPECIAL TYPES OF COMMUNICATION

By now it's apparent that an alphabet is not only our ABCs. An alphabet can be defined as a set of symbols representing the single sounds of a spoken language, by which it is written.

As we have seen, there are other types of writing systems besides alphabets, and there are also other types of communication besides writing.

For example, there is a broad range of sign languages, such as those of the Plains Indians and of the hearing-impaired.

Codes such as the Morse code and semaphore are yet another type of communication. Though they are not written, their signals represent the letters of an alphabet.

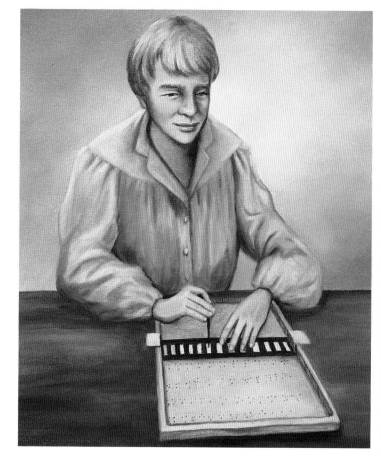

BRAILLE

Blinded by an accident in his early childhood, 15-year-old Louis Braille (1809-1852) invented a system of reading and writing by touch.

A Braille cell consists of six raised dots. By arranging the dots in various combinations, 64 different patterns can be formed.

Braille, a true alphabet, is read by moving the hand from left to right along each line. Readers average about 104-125 words per minute. Some can read 250 words by using both hands.

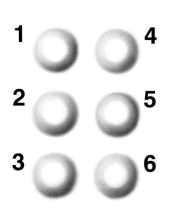

THE ALPHABET ONE FEELS WITH THE FINGERS TO READ

A 1*	B 2	C 3	D 4	E 5	F 6	G 7	H 8	I 9	J 0
K	L	M	N	O	P	Q	R	S	T
U	V	X	Y	Z	and	for	of	the	with
ch	gh	sh	th	wh	ed	er	ou	ow	w
,	;	:	.	en	!	()	"/?	in	"
st	ing	#	ar	'	-				

general accent sign	used for two-celled contractions		italic sign; decimal point	letter sign	capital sign

*WHEN THE FIRST 10 LETTERS ARE PRECEEDED BY THE NUMERIC INDICATOR (#) THE SIGNS HAVE NUMBER VALUE.

MUSIC FOR THE BLIND and Visually Handicapped

The opening bars of Chopin's PRELUDE Opus 28, No. 7

	Key = 3 #'s	Time = 3/4	A	n	d	a	n	t	i	n	o
R.H.	*p*		E			C	D	B		repeat	
L.H.			rest								
R.H.	B										
L.H.											

Braille Transcription

(*Below*) Moon Braille was invented in 1845 by William Moon (1818-1894) of Brighton, England. The embossed Roman letter outline is partly retained and is easily learned by persons who become blind in later life.

(*Bottom*) The Greek alphabet, carved in relief, helped young blind students learn the shape of the Greek letters.

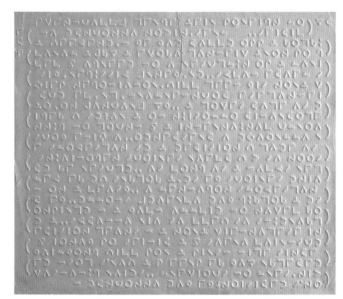

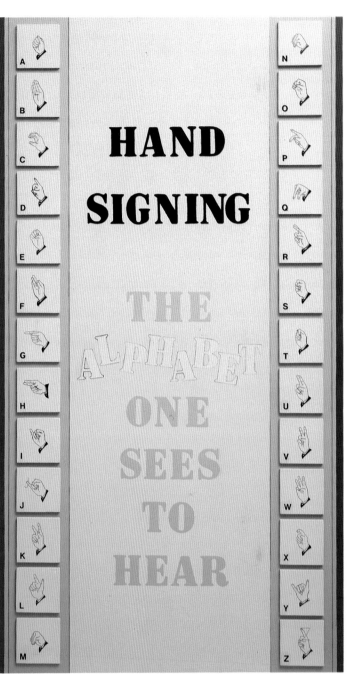

HAND SIGNING

THE ALPHABET ONE SEES TO HEAR

I LOVE YOU

Modern Alphabet Making

Though there are some admirable exceptions, history has shown that it is almost impossible for a culture to produce its own usable writing system from scratch. The lineage of alphabets has shown that they have almost all been "cultural borrowings."

Once a language group has its own written form, however —one elegantly adapted to their own speech and thought —the limits are off as to what they can do with it. An alphabet is a forum for unlimited creativity and expression—for the recording of histories, writing of music, of books, a vehicle for correspondence with each other, and a window on reading. It's also a bridge to other peoples and cultures.

Not everyone enjoys this benefit as yet, however. At least 2000 languages, spoken by a total of more than 300 million people, still lack a written form.

The Summer Institute of Linguistics (SIL) and other organizations encourage alphabet making (usually adaptations of national alphabets), literacy, and Bible translation in such languages.

It's common for speakers of these languages to want them written—to make them more useful. Some groups are fast becoming assimilated into national cultures and languages, a transition that can leave many drifting and rootless.

SIL's alphabet-related work is done in cooperation with national governments, individuals, and existing entities of host countries.

(*Right*) The first book of the New Testament in Navajo, published by the American Bible Society, 1985. (*Below*) Navajo literacy chart.

MATTHEW

Bik'ehgo Hane' Yá'át'éehii

Jesus Christ dabizází yéé

1 ¹ Jesus Christ éí David bits'áádóó oochííłii nilį, áádóó David éí Éíbraham bits'áádóó oochííłii nilį. Kót'éego Jesus Christ bizází yéé nááś da'ahílchį.

2 Éíbraham éí Áízak há yizhchį, áádóó Áízak éí Jéíkab há yizhchį, áádóó bik'iji' Jéíkab éí Júdah dóó bik'isóó há niheezhchį, ³ áádóó ákóne' Téímar éí Píírez índa Zíírah, Júdah bá jishchį, áádóó bik'iji' Píírez éí Hézran há yizhchį, áádóó bik'iji' Hézran éí Ram há yizhchį ⁴ áádóó áadi Ram éí Amínadab há yizhchį, áádóó bik'iji' Amínadab éí Náshon há yizhchį, ákóne' Náshon éí Sálman há yizhchį, ⁵ nááʼákóne' Réíhab éí Bóaz, Sálman bá jishchį, áádóó bik'iji' Ruth éí Obed, Bóaz bá jishchį, áádóó áadi Obed éí Jésii há yizhchį, ⁶ áadi índa Jésii éí David aláahgo naat'áanii há yizhchį.

Áádóó bik'iji' Uráíyah be'asdzáá ńt'é'ígíí éí Sálaman, David bá jishchį, ⁷ áádóó bik'iji' Sálaman éí Rihobóam há yizhchį, ákóne' Rihobóam éí Abáíjah há yizhchį, áádóó áadi Abáíjah éí Éísa há yizhchį, ⁸ áádóó bik'iji' Éísa éí Jeháshafat há yizhchį, ákóne' Jeháshafat éí Jóram há yizhchį, áádóó nááʼákóne' Jóram éí Uzáíyah há yizhchį, ⁹ áádóó áadi Uzáíyah éí Jótham há yizhchį, áádóó bik'iji' Jótham éí Éíhaz há yizhchį, áádóó nááʼákóne' Éíhaz éí Hezekáíyah há yizhchį, ¹⁰ áádóó áadi Hezekáíyah éí Manásah há yizhchį, áádóó bik'iji' Manásah éí Éímon há yizhchį, áádóó nááʼákóne' Éímon éí Josáíyah há yizhchį, ¹¹ áadi índa Bábilangóó ho'disnááh yééędáá Josáíyah éí Jekonáíyah índa bik'isóó há niheezhchį.

¹² Áádóó índa Bábilangóó ho'disnááhdóó bik'iji' Jekonáíyah éí Sheáltiyel há yizhchį, áadi índa Sheáltiyel éí Zerábabel há yizhchį, ¹³ áádóó ákóne' Zerábabel éí Abáíyad há yizhchį, nááʼákóne' Abáíyad éí Eláíyakim há yizhchį, áádóó bik'iji' Eláíyakim éí Éízor há yizhchį, ¹⁴ nááʼákóne' Éízor éí Zéídak há yizhchį, áádóó índa Zéídak éí Éíkim há yizhchį, áádóó bik'iji' Éíkim éí Eláíyad há yizhchį, ¹⁵ nááʼákóne' Eláíyad éí Eliyéízer há yizhchį, áádóó bik'iji' Eliyéízer éí Máthan há yizhchį, índa Máthan éí

1

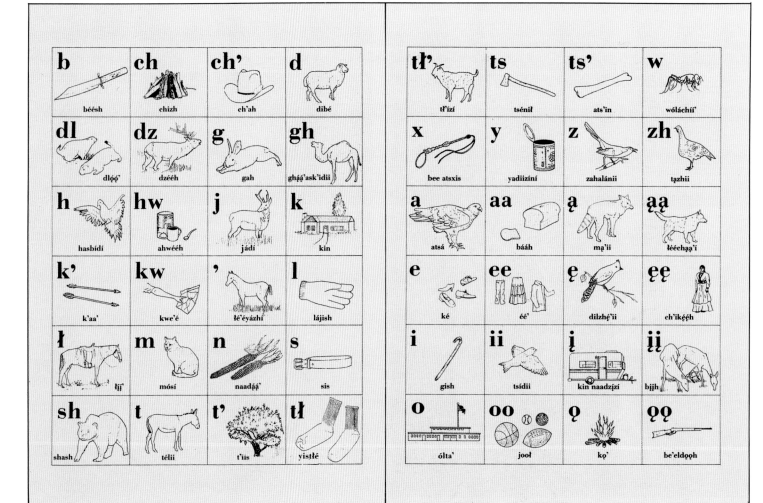

Provision of a scientific alphabet is a debt owed by every scholar to speakers of an illiterate society which he may study.

—Cameron Townsend

Magnificent Team of Scientists, Government and People of Faith

Navajo OF THE UNITED STATES

Organizations interested in American Indians had assumed that all would soon speak English, so no one had made a Navajo alphabet suitable for Navajo literacy.

William Morgan   Robert Young
NAVAJO ALPHABET MAKERS

USA
Navajo

When the U.S. government saw that Navajos resisted English, it turned to bilingual education.
Government linguists John Harrington, Robert Young and William Morgan made a practical alphabet based on the scientific work of Edward Sapir and Zellig Harris. It fit the Navajo language while being close to the writing of English.

The SIL team cooperated with the government in promoting its alphabet and program.

They made primers and reading aids for the schools, and traveled throughout the area teaching literacy.
This encouraged the other organizations working with Navajos to cooperate too.

Morgan and Young also made a bilingual dictionary, which helped SIL people in Bible translation.

Now- there are some 50,000 readers of Navajo, the Navajos are writing their own literature, the Navajo Bible is the backbone of an indigenous Christian movement.

One woman remarked: "English enters my head, but Navajo enters my heart".

Discovering the Phonemes

Phonemes are the distinctive sounds of a spoken language. They are the basis for making an *alphabet*, a set of *letters*, each of which represents one phoneme.

Assigned to the Mixtec language of Mexico, Ken and Evelyn Pike, SIL linguists, had a problem. Ken angered a Mixtec man when he mistakenly told him he would pay *ēēn* (one) peso instead of *ēèn* (nine) pesos. The only difference between the two words was their tone. This was a tonal language, they deduced, like Chinese. Tones were as meaningful as vowels.

But linguistic science was in its infancy and no one could tell him how to figure how many tones there were.

Pike found the clue in the words of the eminent linguist Edward Sapir: "Tones should be compared in context, not in isolation."

Pike searched and prayed for a method that would help others as well. He set up a *tone frame*, a way of comparing tones of a list of words

HEARING PHONEMES THROUGH *THEIR* EARS

Working among the Rotokas people of Papua New Guinea, SIL linguist Skip Firchow had written down the following words: *lagai, nagai, dagai,* and *ragai.* But on reading them back, the people said they could not hear any difference. To them *l, n, d,* and *r* all sounded alike.

It's the same as when English speakers hear no difference between the *l*'s of milk and lettuce, though speakers of some other languages hear them as different sounds.

Each person's ears are tuned to hear only the sounds that distinguish one word from another in his own language. Linguists call these sounds phonemes, and each language has its own set.

In contrast to English, with 45 phonemes, Rotokas has only 11. There are thousands of words in the language. To compensate for the scarcity of phonemes, the words tend to be very long.

PHONEMES BY EYE AND BY EAR

In Australia, SIL linguist Jean Kirton related: "To catch onto the sounds of Yanyuwa, I was always jotting down words I heard people speak, with my eyes glued to the notebook.

"But one time my notebook was tucked away because my hands were full. A friend had just given us some beef. When he said 'goodbye' I saw the tip of his tongue between his teeth.

"That's how I discovered the *interdental* (between-the-teeth) *L* phoneme of the language, which I had missed by not watching."

Since the Yanyuwa used two different *L* sounds in speaking, she included two different *L* letters in the alphabet.

within an unchanging context. Note the example for the word *cu* (it is):

   yucú cú = it is a yoke
   yūcū cú = it is a mountain
   yūcù cú = it is a brush

This frame helped identify the three tonemes (tone phonemes) of Mixtec: high (´), mid (¯), and low (`).

Using this method Pike developed a system of tone analysis which he and his linguist colleagues around the world could use.

(*Above*) Ken Pike and Mixtec co-translator, Angel Merecias, working together in the late 1940s.
(*Right*) Translation and literacy efforts among the Ama people of Papua New Guinea.

In the following pages, several displays will be shown entirely, or in part, as they appear in the *Modern Alphabet Making* section of the museum.

"Why do you write i instead of e?" asked SIL linguist Britten Årsjö while teaching Amas to write their own language.
"It's hard to choose which letter," was the reply.

It was hard to choose because the alphabet had too many letters! The Årsjös had tentatively figured more phonemes than the language actually had, leading to an alphabet with 8 vowels.

But all people, even illiterates, have an intuitive feeling for the phonemes they use in speech.

This came out when Amas began to write their own language, and used only 4 vowels instead of 8.

The Årsjös noticed this, revised their phoneme analysis, and now the alphabet fits the feeling the people have for their own language.

The first step in studying any spoken language is to determine the phonemes.
—H. A. Gleason, Jr

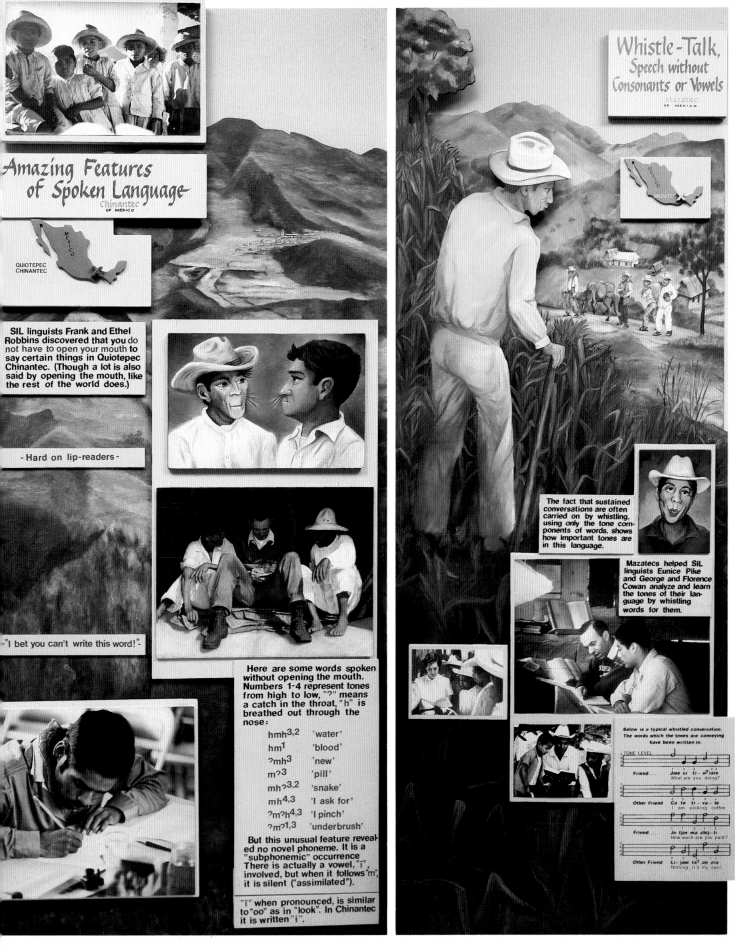

Amazing Features of Spoken Language
Chinantec OF MEXICO

QUIOTEPEC CHINANTEC

SIL linguists Frank and Ethel Robbins discovered that you do not have to open your mouth to say certain things in Quiotepec Chinantec. (Though a lot is also said by opening the mouth, like the rest of the world does.)

- Hard on lip-readers -

-"I bet you can't write this word!"-

Here are some words spoken without opening the mouth. Numbers 1-4 represent tones from high to low, "?" means a catch in the throat, "h" is breathed out through the nose:

hmh^{3,2}	'water'
hm^1	'blood'
?mh^3	'new'
m?^{3}	'pill'
mh?^{3,2}	'snake'
mh^{4,3}	'I ask for'
?m?h^{4,3}	'I pinch'
?m?^{1,3}	'underbrush'

But this unusual feature revealed no novel phoneme. It is a "subphonemic" occurrence. There is actually a vowel, "ɨ", involved, but when it follows "m", it is silent ("assimilated").

"ɨ" when pronounced, is similar to "oo" as in "look". In Chinantec it is written "i".

Whistle-Talk, Speech without Consonants or Vowels
Mazatec OF MEXICO

MEXICO
MAZATEC

The fact that sustained conversations are often carried on by whistling, using only the tone components of words, shows how important tones are in this language.

Mazatecs helped SIL linguists Eunice Pike and George and Florence Cowan analyze and learn the tones of their language by whistling words for them.

Below is a typical whistled conversation. The words which the tones are conveying have been written in.

TONE LEVEL

Friend.... Jme xi ti- n?iain
What are you doing?

Other Friend Ca fe ti - va - te
I am picking coffee

Friend.... Jo tjin ma chij- li
How much are you paid?

Other Friend Li - jme ts? an nia
Nothing, it's my own!

Making the Alphabet

Cameron Townsend, founder of SIL, discovered four different *K* phonemes in Cakchiquel, a Mayan language of Guatemala. He had to find four different ways of writing the *K*'s while staying close to the Spanish alphabet.

Thanks to the Etruscans, the Spanish alphabet is well supplied with *K* letters. The Etruscans had used the Greek *G* (*C*), *K*, and *Q* for one *K* phoneme. This did not make a neat fit to their language, or to Latin, Spanish, or English. But for Cakchiquel it was convenient. The *C* and *Q* alternates for the same sound in Spanish provided Townsend with the four Cakchiquel *K*'s: he represented two of them as *C* and *Qu* in regular type and two in italics.

(*Below*) Cameron and Elvira Townsend in their early days, among the Cakchiquel in Guatemala.

In words pressed onto paper lie man's best hopes of doing something more than merely surviving.

—John Hersey

Adjusting to Dialect Differences
Burum
OF PAPUA NEW GUINEA

The leaders of the Burums asked linguist Soini Olkkonen how to write the phoneme kw, made in back and front of mouth simultaneously:
    a. like English "gu"?
    b. like Pidgin "kw"?
    c. like Kâte "q"?
(Many Burums were taught to read Kâte, a neighboring language, without understanding it.)

First they chose "kw" like Pidgin.

But on testing, Soini found that the Burums of Yakne say "kp" instead of "kw". They pronounce, "kwet", meaning "name", as "kpet". When they saw "kwet" written, they thought it was "kâwet", meaning "sea".

So the committee decided on "q" like Kâte. This suits all dialects because it does not specify which "lip-sound", w or p, goes with the k sound.

Prestige Considerations
Balangao
OF THE PHILIPPINES

The Balangao language could have been written without f, ch, and r, like the Philippine national language, Tagalog.

But when SIL linguist Jo Shetler proposed an alphabet without these, the Balangaos who had studied English in school would not accept it - they were used to the English alphabet.

Since it is just as important to respect the desires of prospective users, as to have a linguistically perfect alphabet, f, ch, and r were included in the Balangao alphabet.

In Balangao,
    f is a variation of b,
    ch of d,
    and r of l.

81

An 'r' or not an 'r'?
Shipibo
OF PERU

Bilingual Education in Peru requires that Indian language alphabets correspond closely to that of Spanish.

200 years ago Spanish Catholic missionaries set the pattern for Shipibo by writing it according to Spanish usage.

But they did not hear one of the sounds - a "retroflexed" consonant (tongue-tip-turned-back), because Spanish has no retroflexed sounds.

Some American non-linguists heard it, because English has a retroflexed sound, "r". They wrote this Shipibo sound as they heard it: 'shr'.

But Spanish readers could not relate the Shipibo sound to "r", because Spanish "r" sounds quite different.

Shipibo retroflexed sound and English "r"   Spanish "r"

Shipibo retroflexed sound and English "r"

SIL linguist Jim Loriot decided to write the retroflexion with 2 dots rather than with "r": 'sh'.

Now school children have no problem reading both Shipibo and Spanish.

Shipibo face-painting stick

Tone Marks – Like Road Signs
Yacouba
OF CÔTE D'IVOIRE

Côte d' Ivoire
Yacouba (Dan)

Finally - punctuation! Before a syllable* it shows the level to start on, and after, if a contour tone, how to end:

" (quote mark)	=	high tone
' (apostrophe)	=	mid-high
no mark	=	mid
- (dash)	=	falling
= (equals sign)	=	low

*Most words have only one syllable

The Dans intensely desired to read their language, yet few could, because tones were not written.

"But how should we write contour tones on a typewriter?" wondered SIL linguist Margrit Bolli.

Accent marks were out – French, the national language uses them for vowel qualities, as does Dan. Use numbers? The people called it a "math nightmare". Extra letters q, j, x? "A language from Mars," they said.

LIST OF KEY WORDS WITH TONES MARKED IS ON LEFT; WORDS UNMARKED FOR TONE ARE ON RIGHT. EACH STUDENT COMPARES SOUND OF AN UNMARKED WORD WITH KEY WORDS BY WHISTLING, THEN MARKS HIS WORD.

A pleased reader: "Those marks are like road signs to tell us which way to go".
Now thousands read and write Dan, and the system is official for other languages as well.

TAI DAM
THREE ALPHABETS FOR ONE LANGUAGE

Scattered to the four winds, different groups of the Tai Dam of Vietnam have become literate in different alphabets.

To begin with, they have their own Indic-type alphabet, the 1300-year old Tai Dam alphabet, of which they are proud. One man arriving in Iowa requested: "Mr. President, please do not make us give up our alphabet."

In other parts of Vietnam, children learned the Vietnamese type of Roman alphabet. Others learned the Laotian alphabet in Laos. Some went to France and the U.S., lands which use the Roman alphabet.

SIL linguists, making books in the Tai Dam language, use all three alphabets to accommodate the different backgrounds: Tai Dam, Lao, and Roman. Computer technology is used for typesetting. The Vietnamese-Roman is typed in and the computer automatically transliterates in the other two.

(*Below*) A page from a reading primer and *Selections from the Life of Christ* using the three alphabets of the Tai Dam language.

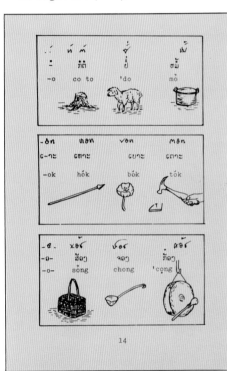

Literacy

VAGLA OF GHANA

ROOFTOP LITERACY FITS THE CULTURE

After learning the language, making an alphabet, translating the New Testament, and starting to teach reading, SIL linguists Marj Crouch and Pat Herbert left the rest of the literacy work to the Vaglas.

Their interest had just begun when a period of civil unrest disrupted the Vagla world. It was questionable whether interest in literacy would start again.

Jebenee Kiipo, who had come to faith through reading the Bible, discovered that many Vaglas wanted to learn to read. He revived the literacy program and became its supervisor, sponsored by the village chiefs.

Every evening the housetops would hum with reading classes. (The Vaglas do everything on their roofs.)

The newspaper they write and publish once expressed their motivation: "Every Vagla should try to learn to read, because reading . . . will help us to know our Father God."

An alphabet is for reading and writing a language. But these activities are foreign to a society whose language has not been written. To be accepted, literacy must find a cultural niche, and fill a felt need. For the Vagla, this means starting on the roof.

Awakened by the Bells

Mamanwa
OF THE PHILIPPINES

What could induce the Mamanwas to try literacy? Fishing seemed to be their only interest, and reading would not help catch fish!

This was the concern of Lilia Castro, Filipina literacy specialist sent to the Mamanwas by a Philippine organization. She tried to think of what they valued besides fish.

Then she remembered their fascination with the tiny brass bells the distant Tbolis make. She offered these as prizes to anyone learning a chapter of the Mamanwa primer.

It worked! 2 grandmothers were the first to try. To everyone's surprise they learned 3 chapters, earned 3 bells each, then kept on going.

Many more followed suit. The Mamanwas have now built a "Timothy Training Center"* to help meet the needs that fish do not meet.

*taken from the Bible verse, 2 Timothy 2:2 – "The things which you have heard, the same entrust to faithful men who will be able to teach others also".

A Pencil Opens a Door
Cuiba OF COLOMBIA

A pencil lying on the desk of SIL linguist Marie Berg caught the eye of a 12 year old boy.
"Will you give me this?" he asked.
It was granted.
"Can you teach me to use it?"

This is how literacy started among the nomadic Cuibas, locked into their own little world, with no way out. In about 20 hours this youth had learned to read and write his own language, and began to write stories.

When he read those to his kinsmen, they were amazed. They all gathered to see and hear, asking him to teach them.

At first writing was a game. Later, many established themselves near a school and planted gardens, so they could attend classes.
The Colombian government took notice and is training Cuiba teachers.

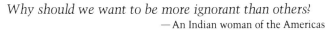

Why should we want to be more ignorant than others?
— An Indian woman of the Americas

THE AGUARUNA OF PERU
LITERACY BRINGS DEFENSE

While preparing dinner at their home a hundred miles from a road, Millie Larson and Jeanne Grover were visited by a delegation of feathered Aguarunas. "We have come to buy a teacher," they announced.

They hoped that education would give their children skills to deal with the outside world.

"We have no teacher for sale," they were told, "but choose some of your bright young people and we will see that they are trained to be your teachers."

Since 1953 a bilingual training school has been conducted by the Peruvian government and SIL, to train jungle Indian teachers. More than 10,000 Aguarunas have benefited.

Once some unscrupulous non-Indian settlers displayed an impressive-looking document and claimed they had a deed to some Aguaruna land. An educated Aguaruna studied it for a moment and conceded, "It is a fine Singer sewing machine warranty!"

(*Above*) Aguaruna fathers enrolling their children in a bilingual school.
(*Below*) Participants in the teacher training course in the Peruvian rain forest.

86

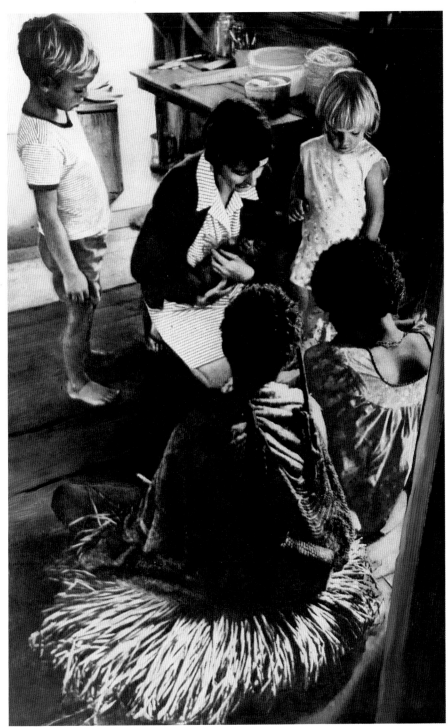

THE BINUMARIEN OF PAPUA NEW GUINEA

AN ENDANGERED SPECIES

Like the world's endangered species of birds and animals, some groups of humans are also threatened with extinction.

For the Binumarien of Papua New Guinea it was ideas, not enemies, that were destroying them. Their numbers were down to 112 when SIL linguists Des and Jenny Oatridge first went to them.

The Binumarien had come to believe that God had not originally created woman, but that he had turned a man into a woman as punishment. Conjugal relations were considered cursed, and childbirth a danger to the community.

But after an alphabet was made and Bible translation began, excitement ran through the villages over the Genesis account of creation—written in their own language. It said, "God made man in his own image—male and female created he them."

So womanhood was good! Home life was consequently transformed. In the 20 years following, the number of Binumarien tripled.

THE GUAHIBO OF COLOMBIA
THE PEN IS MIGHTIER THAN BOW AND ARROW

Outsiders were bringing their cattle into the area of the Guahibos, damaging their manioc plants, and straining their patience. Occasionally an arrow, shot in retaliation, was found in a cow. But Marcelino Sosa had a better way.

After SIL linguists Vic and Riena Kondo formed an alphabet, Marcelino started a bilingual newspaper. The newspaper called on Indians and ranchers to unite for the common good.

As a forum for airing complaints, it helped work out land problems and secure benefits for the area. It is the only newspaper in the state. It is produced entirely by the Guahibos on a silk-screen mimeograph, in a thatch-roofed hut, two days' walk from the nearest dirt road. It is registered with the government. The editor, Sosa, is nationally recognized. The alphabet has provided ethnic cohesion to the Guahibos; it is a cultural anchor in a sea of change.

THE TICUNA

Deep in the Amazon rainforest, the Ticuna have experienced internal transformation—the result of cooperation between concerned governments, SIL linguists, and the Ticuna themselves.

It's a classic "before and after" story. Before, the Ticuna were continually exploited and always in debt; today they are trained in a variety of occupations, know how to read and write, and carry out medical responsibilities.

In earlier days most money was spent on alcohol; today many own their own land and run a variety of industries.

Once they were known only for blowgun dart poison; today they have built a model community with total self-government.

Frequent machete fights and drunken puberty rites once made it a dangerous place to live. Today the Ticuna are proud of their culture, their language, and their achievements.

The Roots
AND
The Fruit
OF Ticuna
OF PERU, BRAZIL,
AND COLOMBIA

TICUNA
PERU

BILINGUAL TEACHER AND OCCUPATIONAL TRAINING SCHOOLS FOR JUNGLE INDIAN LEADERS

Government Land Grant and other assistance

Training of Ticuna Authors and Translators

COOPERATIVE

CATTLE AND CROPS

BIBLE STUDY FROM TICUNA TRANSLATION

PERUVIAN GOVERNMENT PROGRAMS FOR ITS MINORITY LANGUAGE GROUPS

TICUNA INITIATIVE IN DEVELOPING THEIR OWN CULTURE

LINGUISTIC WORK: ALPHABET, LITERACY, AND BIBLE TRANSLATION

Typesetting for Today's Alphabets

As each language in the world is unique, so is its alphabet. Choosing what characters to use in a language's alphabet can be a complicated process.

In many areas around the world where SIL linguists work, the national languages use the Roman alphabet. Linguists then use Roman characters to form new alphabets. However, often the Roman characters alone cannot adequately represent the unique sounds of a language. Diacritics (marks added to letters to change their pronunciation) can then be used to expand the number of sounds that can be written. They are also used to mark tone or stress.

In other areas the major languages use non-Roman alphabets that are very old. The people treasure their way of writing. However, there has been no way of typesetting them for the minority languages. Now SIL computer specialists are designing typography for these scripts.

In the southern Philippines many Muslim speakers of minority languages use the Arabic alphabet. But some of their characters differ slightly from those used in the Middle East and North Africa. To address this, SIL technicians are developing a computer program that adapts the Arabic alphabet to these minority languages.

SIL is now able to prepare camera-ready copy in the following alphabets: Devanagari, Ethiopic, Greek, Tai Dam, Laotian, Arabic, and Roman with numerous diacritics.

Research and development continue adapting new and ancient alphabets to printing technology. It's all part of the process of being alphabet makers.

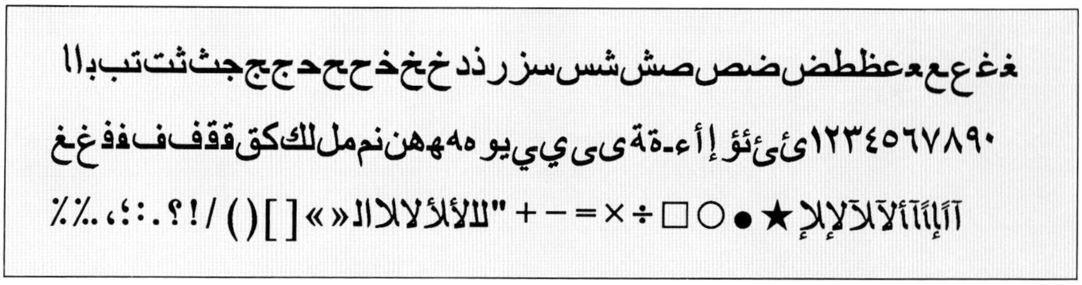

Arabic

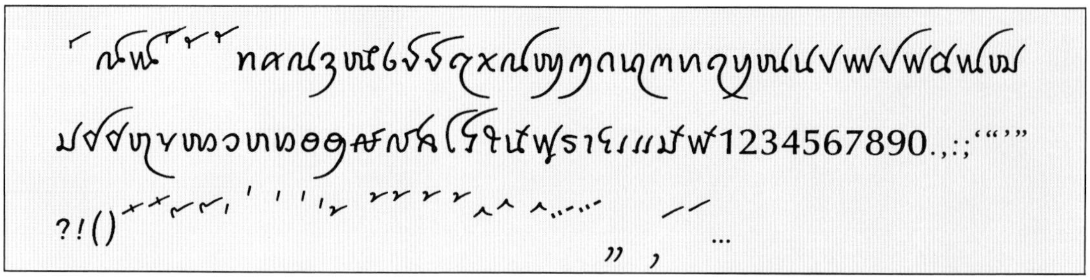

Tai Dam

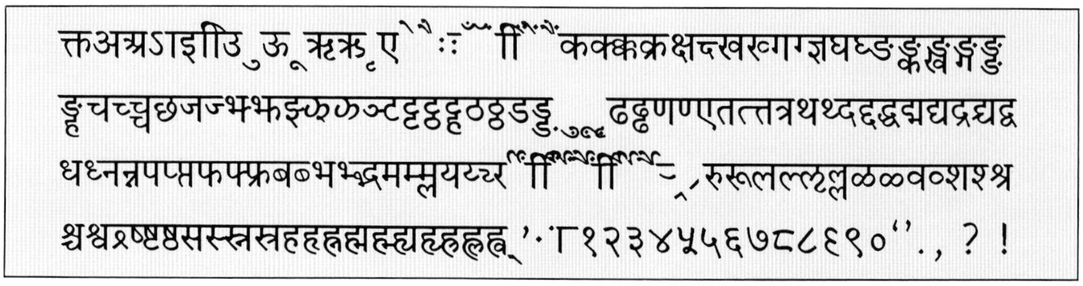

Devanagari

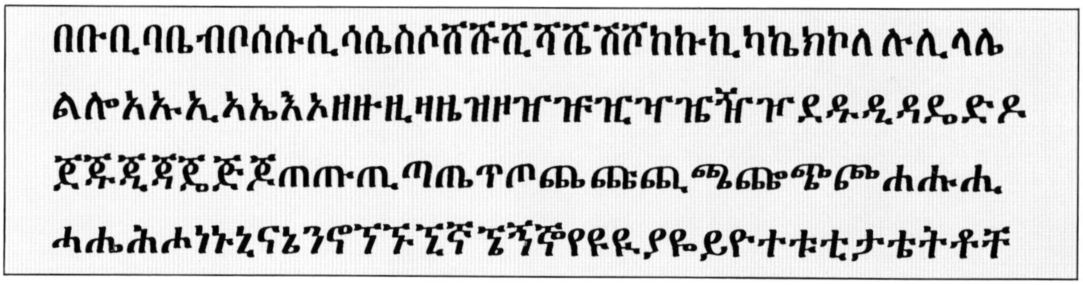

Ethiopic

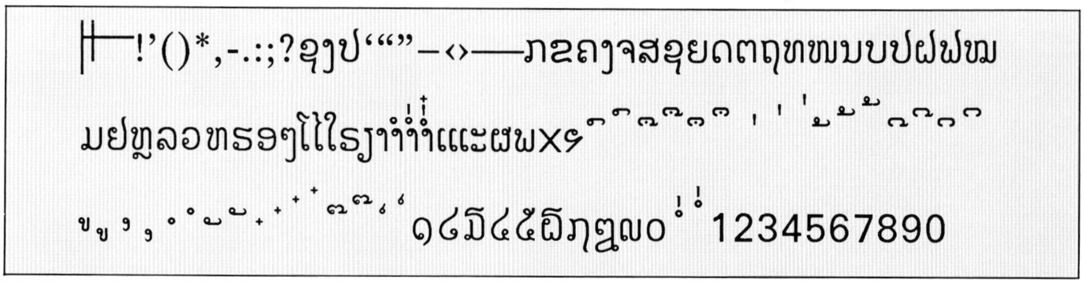

Laotian

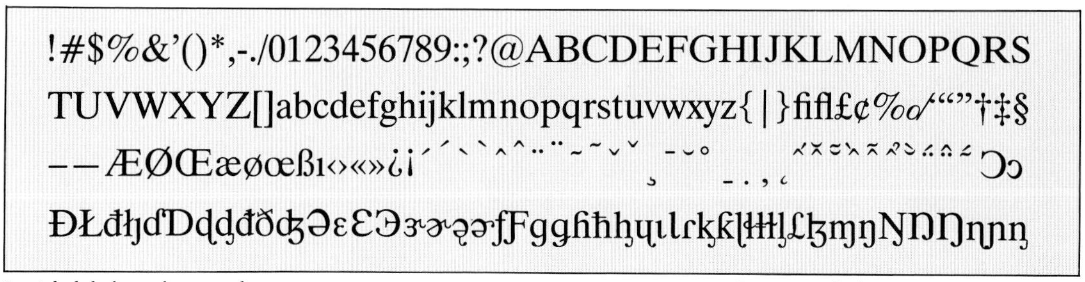

Partial alphabets shown only.

Roman with diacritics

Volunteers Who Contributed to the Development of the Musuem of the Alphabet

Heather Abbott
Doris Anderson
Lambert Anderson
Lorrie Anderson
Britten Arsjo
Soren Arsjo
Lil Aspenson

Jerry Bair
Virginia Baker
Myra Lou Barnard
Lieselotte Bartlett
Rodney Bartlett
Alma Bascom
Harry Bascom
Louise Bass
Alan Baughman
Mary Beekman
Deborah Beery
Ann Belk
Henderson Belk
Marie Berg
Dick Bergman
Nancy Bergman
Cindy Bitterman
Betty Blair
Dorothy Blair
Marcus Blair
David Blood
Doris Blood
Turner Blount
Margrit Bolli
Pat Bonnell
Wayne Borthwick
James Brase
Julie Brown
Merlin Brown
Alan Buseman
Karen Buseman
Barbara Butler
Dan Butler
Roy Butters

Cornell Capa
Bub Catlett
John Chao
Ric Chin
Eva Claffee
Jim Claffee
Nancy Clark
John Cleaveland
John Cornyn
Florrie Cowan

George Cowan
Doris Cox
Marjorie Crofts
Marjorie Crouch
Carroll Crowell

Willis Dalby
Frieda DeKoning
Ron DeKoning
Sue Demick
David Denyer
Beverly Baker Dinsmore
Bob Donaldson
Jean Donaldson

Artemisa Echegoyen
Faye Edgerton
Joyce Edwards
Ted Engel
Bev Entz
Harry Eshbach

Peter Fast
William Ferguson
Harriet Fields
Jackie Firchow
Skip Firchow
Jay Fippinger
Jan Forster
Kirk Franklin
Eugenia Fuller

Elizabeth Gibbes
Lynn Gibbs
Terry Gibbs
Merlin Giddings
Dominique Gotsch
Diana Green
Harold Green
Mary Kathleen Greene
Barbara Grimes
Joe Grimes
Jeanne Grover
Elke Gustafsson
Uwe Gustafsson

Jack Haan
Bill Hanna
Regina Hannagan

Jim Hathaway
June Hathersmith
Marion Heaslip
Doug Helms
Patricia Herbert
Don Hesse
Alice Hester
Cal Hibbard
Faith Hill
Mary Beth Hinson
Emilie Hipp
Holly Hong
Steve Hong
Ralph Hopper
Paulette Hopple
Don Horneman
Jane Horneman
Sharon Horning
Joe Horvath

Christine Jackson
Dorothy Jackson
Evangelyn Jackson
Bert Johnson
Fred Johnson
Martha Johnson
Charles Jurgensen

Grace Kelso
Wally Kennicutt
Isabel Kerr
Jean Kirton
Riena Kondo
Vic Kondo
Alex Koval
Hattie Kneeland

Millie Larson
Karen Lewis
Richard Long
Jim Loriot
Roy Lowry

James Magnuson
Harry McArthur
Lucille McArthur
Sharon McCririe
Carolyn Miller
Helen Miller

Jeanne Miller
John Miller
Jack Milligan
Pat Milligan
Jesse Moore
Mrs. Muckenfusz
Rose Muno

Yasuko Nagai
Helen Neuenswander
Linda Niehoff

Desmond Oatridge
Jennifer Oatridge
Kirby O'Brien
Kaija Olkkonen
Soini Olkkonen

Wanda Pace
Valentine Parnakian
Heather Patrick
Nora Pestana
Alice Peterson
Viretta Petro
Tambi Pharayra
Eunice Pike
Evie Pike
Ken Pike
Merrill Piper
Kay Pittman
Richard Pittman
Martin Popp
Agnes Poppen

Peggy Richards
Dave Robbins
Ethel Robbins
Frank Robbins
Vivian Robbins
Anthony Rossi
Sanna Rossi
Beth Rupprecht

Rachel Saint
Cliff Salisbury
Bill Sasnett
Marietta Scherick
Christopher Schirk
Miriam Schnittker
Lynn Silvernale
Frank Smarik
Paul Smith

Arthur Speck
Carolyn Steele
Richard Steele
Vivie Stiteler
Ernest Stoffel
Jean Surratt
Harriet Swauger
Wesley Swauger

Margaret Sheffler
Bob Shelby
Todd Shelby
Jenny Shen
Ann Shephard
Jo Shetler
Hue Kan Shi

David Tani
Chris Tatios
Margaret Taylor
Tim Toba
Cameron Townsend
Elaine Townsend
Mildred Townsend
Martha Duff Tripp

Randy Valentine
Steve Van Rooy

John Walton
Lillian Ward
Ernie Warnick
Grace Watkins
Klaus Wedekind
Jeff Weir
Ida Wells
Peggy Wendell
Stella Whitehouse
Mary Ruth Wise
Paul Wyse
Peggy Wyse

Robert Young

Don Ziemer
Immie Ziemer

Bibliography

Abegian, M. 1948. *Istoria Drevnear-mianskoi Literatury* 1. Yerevan: s.n.

Abercrombie, Thomas J. 1964. "Behind the Veil of Troubled Yemen." *National Geographic* 125.3 (March).

Abramson, Rebecca, trans. 1961. *The Orion Book of the Written Word*. New York: Orion Press.

Algeo, John. 1972. *Problems in the Origins and Development of the English Language*. New York: Harcourt Brace Jovanovich.

Allott, Stephen. 1974. *Alcuin of York: His Life and Letters*. York, England: William Sessions.

"Alphabet." *Chambers Encyclopedia*. 1. 1959. London: George Newnes.

"Alphabet, Hebrew." *Encyclopaedia Judaica*. 2. 1971. Jerusalem, Israel: Keter Pub. House.

American Foundation for the Blind. N.d. *Louis Braille*. New York: American Foundation for the Blind.

American Foundation for the Blind. [1968] *Understanding Braille*. New York: American Foundation for the Blind.

Anderson, Charles R. 1969. *Lettering*. New York: Van Nostrand Reinhold.

Angrawala, Vasudeu Sharana. 1953. *India as Known to Panini: A Study of the Cultural Material in Ashtadhyayi*. Lucknow: Univ. of Lucknow.

Apel, W., and Ralph T. Daniel. 1961. *The Harvard Brief Dictionary of Music*. New York: Pocket Books.

Arabian American Oil Co. 1969. *Aramco Handbook: Oil and the Middle East*. Dhahran, Saudi Arabia: Arabian American Oil Co.

Ascher, Marcia, and Robert Ascher. 1975. "The Quipu as a Visible Language." *Visible Language* 9.4 (Autumn).

Asimov, Isaac. 1968. *Words from History*. Boston: Houghton Mifflin.

Asratian, G. (R. Mazelev, photo.) 1973. *Yerevan and its Environs*. Leningrad: Aurora Art Pub.

"Austro-Asiatic Language." 1974. *The New Encyclopaedia Britannica*. Micropaedia 1.

Autry, Hugh R. 1941. *New Echota: Birthplace of the American Indian Press*. Washington, D.C.: National Park Service.

Auvray, Paul, Pierre Poulain, and Albert Blaise. 1963. *Sacred Languages*. J. Tester, trans. New York: Hawthorn Books.

Aveni, Anthony, F. 1975. *Archaeoastronomy in Pre-Columbian America*. Austin: Univ. of Texas Press.

Aveni, Anthony F. 1977. "Astronomy in Ancient Mesoamerica." In *In Search of Ancient Astronomies*. Krupp, E.C., ed. Garden City, N.Y.: Doubleday.

Aveni, Anthony F. 1977. *Native American Astronomy*. Austin: Univ. of Texas Press.

Aveni, Anthony F. N.d. *Archaeastronomy in the Maya Region: 1970-1980*. S.I.: s.n.

Azzi, Robert. 1980. "Saudi Arabia: the Kingdom and its Power." *National Geographic* 158.3 (Sept.)

Barnett, M. Robert. 1974. "Braille." *The New Encyclopaedia Britannica*. Macropaedia 3.

Barraclough, Geoffrey, ed. 1978. *The Times Atlas of World History*. Maplewood, N. J.: Hammond.

Bates, Marston. 1956. "Ifalik: Lonely Paradise of the South Seas." *National Geographic* 109.4 (April).

Bateson, M. C. 1967. *Arabic Language Handbook*. Washington, D.C.: The Center for Applied Linguistics.

Bell, Donald. 1972. "Reading by Touch." *Braille Monitor* (June).

Bennett, Ross. S., ed. 1982. *Lost Empires, Living Tribes*. Washington, D.C.: National Geographic Society.

Benson, Elizabeth P. 1967. *The Maya World*. New York: Thomas Y. Crowell.

Benson, Elizabeth P. 1973. *Mesoamerican Writing Systems*. Washington, D.C.: Dumbarton Oaks Research Library and Collections, Trustee for Harvard University.

Berberi, Dilaver. 1975. *Arabic in a Nutshell*. Montclair, N.J.: Funk & Wagnalls.

Bergsträsser, Gotthelf. 1983. *Introduction to the Semitic Languages*. Peter T. Daniels, trans. Winona Lake, Ind.: Eisenbrauns.

Berlin, Heinrich. 1977. *Signos y Significados en las Inscripciones Mayas*. Guatemala: Inst. Nacl. del Patrimonio Cultural.

Biblical Illustrator Magazine. 1985. (Summer Issue.)

Blunden, Caroline, and Mark Elvin. 1983. *Cultural Atlas of China*. New York: Facts on File.

Bolinger, Dwight. 1972. *Regarding Language*. New York: Harcourt Brace Jovanovich.

The Book of Popular Science. 1957. New York: The Groilier Soc.

Bowra, C. M., and the editors of Time-Life Books. 1965. *Classical Greece*. New York: Time-Life Books.

Boyer, David S. 1967. "Micronesia: the Americanization of Eden." *National Geographic* 131.5 (May).

Brander, Bruce., 1987. "No More Nomadic Life." *World Vision* (April-May).

Bricker, Victoria R., ed. 1981. *Supplement to the Handbook of Middle American Indians*. Vol. 1, *Archaeology*. Jeremy A. Sabluff, vol. ed. Austin, Texas: Univ. of Texas Press.

The British and Foreign Bible Society. N.d. *The Story of the English Bible*. Bedford, England: Henry Burt & Son.

The British Library. 1977. "Initial U" [postcard]. England: The British Library Board.

Britten, Benjamin, and I. Holst. 1968. *The Wonderful World of Music*. New York: Doubleday.

Brown, T. Julian. 1974. "Punctuation." *The New Encyclopaedia Britannica*. Macropaedia 15.

Budge, E. A. Wallis. 1975. *Ancient Egyptian Language*. Chicago: Ares Pub.

Burwash, Nathaniel. 1911. "The Gift to a Nation of Written Language." *Transaction, Sect. II. Papers for 1911*. S.I.

Buxton, David. 1970. *The Abyssinians*. New York: Praeger Pub.

The Cambridge Medieval History 3. N.d. Cambridge, England: Cambridge Univ. Press.

Caputo, Robert. 1983. "Ethiopia: Revolution in an Ancient Empire." *National Geographic* 163.5 (May).

Carroll, David. 1972. "The Taj Mahal: India Under the Moguls." *Newsweek*.

Carroll, John. N.d. "James Evans: The Planter of Methodist Missions in Rupert's Land." *Canadian Methodist Magazine*.

Carter, T. Donald. (Walter A. Weber, artist.) 1956. "Stalking Central Africa's Wildlife." *National Geographic* 110.2 (Aug.).

Carter, Thomas Francis, and L. Carrington Goodrich. N.d. *Invention of Printing in China and its Spread Westward*. S.I.: Roland Press.

Casson, Lionel, and the editors of Time-Life Books. 1965. *Ancient Egypt*. New York: Time-Life Books.

Catherwood, Frederick. N.d. [Reproduction of a painting of a Mayan temple]. Mexico City: Museum of Anthropology.

Chafe, Wallace L., and Jack Frederick Kilpatrick. N.d. *Inconstencies in Cherokee Spelling*. S.I.: s.n.

Chen, Matthew Y. 1986. Review of *The Chinese Language: Fact and Fantasy*, by John DeFrancis. *Language* 62.3.

Cherokee alphabet. 1967. [Postcard]. Cherokee, N.C. : Underwood and Sharpe.

Cherokee seal. S.I.: s.n.

Chiera, Edward. 1938. *They Wrote on Clay*. Chicago: Univ. of Chicago Press.

Chomsky, William. 1957. *Hebrew the Eternal Language*. Philadelphia: Jewish Pub. Soc. of America.

Claiborn, Robert, and the editors of Time-Life Books. 1974. *The Birth of Writing*. New York: Time-Life Books.

Cobb, Stanwood. 1963. *Islamic Contributions to Civilization*. Washington, D.C.: Avalon Press.

Coe, Michael D. 1968. *America's First Civilization*. 3rd ed. New York: American Heritage.

Coe, Michael D. 1984. *Mexico*. 3rd ed. New York: Thames & Hudson.

Collaer, Paul, and Albert Vander Linden. 1968. *Historical Atlas of Music*. Allen Miller, trans. Cleveland: World Pub.

Craighead, Frank, Jr., and John Craighead. 1966. "Trailing Yellowstone's Grizzlies by Radio." *National Geographic* 130.2 (Aug.).

"Cree." 1974. *The New Encyclopaedia Britannica*. Micropaedia 3.

Cross, Frank Moore, Jr., and D.N. Freedman. 1952. *Early Hebrew Orthography: A Study of the Epigraphic Evidence*. New Haven, Conn.: American Oriental Society.

Crump, C. G., and E. F. Jacob, eds. 1932. *The Legacy of the Middle Ages*. London: Oxford Univ. Press.

Dalby, David. 1970. *Language and History in Africa*. New York: Africana Pub.

Dalby, David. 1986. *Africa and the Written Word*. Paris: Imprimeries Réunis de Senlis.

Davidson, A. B. 1874. *An Introductory Hebrew Grammar*. Edinburgh: T. & T. Clark.

Davidson, Basil. 1966. *African Kingdoms*. New York: Time.

Davidson, Margaret. 1971. *Louis Braille: The Boy Who Invented Books for the Blind*. New York: Scholastic Book Service.

DeFrancis, John. 1984. *The Chinese Language: Fact and Fantasy*. Honolulu: Univ. of Hawaii Press.

"Deciphering the Indus Valley Script, Part II." 1980. *India News* (Jan.).

Diakanoff, Igor Mikhailovich. 1974. "Hamito-Semitic Languages." *The New Encyclopaedia Britannica*. Macropaedia 8.

Diringer, David. N.d. *Writing and the Alphabet*. Tel-Aviv: Museum Haaretz.

Diringer, David. 1953. *Staples Alphabet Exhibition: Sponsored and Arranged by Staples Press*. London: Staples Press.

Diringer, David. [1962]. *Writing*. New York: Praeger.

Diringer, David. 1968. *The Alphabet: a Key to the History of Mankind*. 3rd ed. London: Hutchinson.

Diringer, David. 1974. "Alphabets." *Encyclopedia Britannica*. Macropaedia 1.

Doblhofer, E. 1961. *Voices in Stone*. Mervyn Savill, trans. New York: Viking Press.

Doig, Desmond. 1966. "Sherpaland: My Shangri-la." *National Geographic* 130.4 (Oct.).

Douglas, J. D., ed. 1980. *The Illustrated Bible Dictionary* 1. Wheaton, Ill.: Tyndale House Pub.

Ducoff, Helen. 1979. *How to Read Hebrew (And Love It!)*. Concord, Mass.: Heinle & Heinle.

Edey, Maitland A., and the editors of Time-Life Books. 1974. *The Sea Traders*. New York: Time Life Books.

Edwards, Lizzie. N.d. "Kamaa Chiinipahaakpane Aniyuu Atihkwa: I Wish He Had Killed That Caribou." In *Hard Times*. Clara Cooper, ed. Chibougamau: Cree Publications Meroz.

Edwards, Mike. (David Alan Harvey, photo.) 1980. "Tunisia: Sea, Sand, Success." *National Geographic* 157.2 (Feb).

Ellis, William S. (George F. Mobley, photo.) "Lebanon: Little Bible Land in the Crossfire of History." *National Geographic* 137.2 (Feb).

Englebert, Victor. 1968. "Trek by Mule among Morocco's Berbers." *National Geographic* 133.6 (June).

Evans, James. 1837. *The Speller and Interpreter in Indian and English*. New York: D. Franshaw.

Fairbank, Alfred. 1970. *Story of Handwriting Origins/Development*. New York: Watson-Gupstill Pub.

Fairservis, Walter A., Jr. 1983. "The Script of the Indus Valley Civilization." *Scientific American* 248.3 (March).

Feeling, Durbin, and William Pulte, eds. 1975. *Cherokee-English Dictionary*. Tahlequah, Okla.: Cherokee Nation of Oklahoma.

Ferguson, William, and John Royce. 1984. *Mayan Ruins in Central America in Color*. Albuquerque, N.M.: Univ. of N.M. Press.

Fiero, Charles. N.d. *Ojibwa Syllabics*. Unpublished.

Fisher, Leonard Everett. 1978. *Alphabet Art: Thirteen ABC's from around the World*. New York: Four Winds Press.

Flannery, Kent V., and Joyce Marcus, eds. 1983. *The Cloud People: Divergent Evolution of the Zapotec and Mixtec Civilization*. New York: Academic Press.

Franklin, William L. 1973. "High, Wild World of the Vicuña." *National Geographic* 143.1 (Jan.).

Friedrich, Johannes. 1957. *Extinct Languages*. Frank Gaynor, trans. New York: Philosophical Library.

Froncek, Thomas, ed. 1969. *The Horizon Book of the Arts of China*. New York: American Heritage.

Fry, Edmond. 1799. *Pantographia: Containing Accurate Copies of All the Known Alphabets in the World*. London: Cooper and Wilson.

Gair, James. W. 1986. "Alphabet." *Collier's Encyclopedia* 1.

Garbini, Giovanni. 1979. *Storia e Problemi del'Epigrafia Semitica*. Napoli: Institute Orientale.

Gelb, Ignace J. 1963. *A Study of Writing*. Rev. ed. Chicago: Univ. of Chicago Press.

The Geneva Bible [folio page]. 1560.

Gerster, Georg. 1970. "Searching out Medieval Churches in Ethiopia's Wilds." *National Geographic* 138.6 (Dec.).

Gibbon, David. 1979. *China: A Picture Book to Remember Her By*. New York: Crescent Books.

Goldenthal, Allan B. 1978. *Think Chinese—Speak Chinese*. New York: Regents.

Goldron, Romain. 1968. *Byzantine and Medieval Music*. New York: H. S. Studtman.

Goldstücker, Theodor. 1965. *Panini*. Varanasi, India: Chowkhamba, Sanskrit Series Office.

Gordon, Cyrus, N.d. *Cracking the Code* [Tablet]. Philadelphia: Univ. of Penn Museum.

Grey, Ian, ed. 1970. *The Horizon History of Russia*. New York: American Heritage.

Grimes, Barbara F., ed. 1988. *Ethnologue: Languages of the World*. 11th ed. Dallas: Summer Institute of Linguistics.

Grollenberg, Luc. H. 1959. *Shorter Atlas of the Bible*. S.I.: Thomas Nelson and Son.

Grosvenor, Gilbert M. 1960. "When the President Goes Abroad." *National Geographic* 117.5 (May).

Grosvenor, Melville Bell. 1959. "Around the World and the Calendar with the Geographic." *National Geographic* 116.6 (Dec.).

Grove, Noel. (Steve Raymer, photo.) 1979. "Volatile North Yemen." *National Geographic* 156.2 (Aug.)

Gutterman, Leon, ed. 1976. *God's Wisdom and the Holy Bible*. Beverly Hills, Calif.: The Wisdom Society.

Hadas, Moses, and the editors of Time-Life Books. 1965. *Imperial Rome*. New York: Time-Life Books.

Hager, Giuseppe. 1972. *An Explanation of the Elementary Characters of the Chinese*. Menston, Yorkshire, England: The Scholar Press.

Halle, Morris. 1972. *Language by Ear and by Eye: The Relationships Between Speech and Reading*. Kavanagh, ed. Cambridge, Mass.: MIT Press.

Hanley, Charles J. 1987. "Technology a Threat to Eskimo Language." *Charlotte Observer* (Sept. 20).

Harris, Joseph E., ed. 1974. *Pillars in Ethiopian History*. Washington, D.C.: Howard Univ. Press.

Harris, Zellig. 1945. "Navajo Phonology and Hoijer's Analysis." *International Journal of American Linguistics* 11:239-246.

Hedlund, Monica. 1983. [Letter from Uppsala Universitetsbibliotek]. Uppsala, Sweden.

Helfman, Elizabeth. N.d. *Signs and Symbols Around the World*. S.I.: s.n.

Henderson, John S. 1981. *The World of the Ancient Maya*. Ithaca, N.Y.: Cornell Univ. Press.

Henthorn, William E. 1971. *History of Korea*. New York: The Free Press.

The Heritage of Islam. 1982. San Francisco: Calif. Academy of Sciences.

Hertz, Solange, trans. 1966. *Rhodes of Vietnam*. Westminster, Md.: The Newman Press.

Ifrah, Georges. 1985. *From One to Zero*. Lowell Bair, trans. New York: Viking Penguin.

Illustrated Family Encyclopedia of the Living Bible. 1967. Chicago: San Francisco Productions.

Irwin, Keith Gordon. 1958. *The Romance of Writing*. London: David Dobson.

Jacobson, Doranne Wilson. 1977. "Purdah in India: Life Behind the Veil." *National Geographic* 152.2 (Aug.).

James, A.H.M., and Elizabeth Monroe. [1935] 1960. *A History of Ethiopia*. Oxford: The Clarendon Press.

Jensen, Hans. 1969. *Sign, Symbol and Script*. New York: G. P. Putnam's Sons.

Joint Uniform Braille Committee. 1959. *English Braille*. American ed. Louisville, Ky.: American Printing House for the Blind.

Jordan, Robert Paul. (Harry N. Naltchayan, photo.) 1978. "The Proud Armenians." *National Geographic* 153.6 (June).

Kaplan, Marion. 1974. "Twilight of the Arab Dhow." *National Geographic* 146.3 (Sept.).

Katzner, Kenneth. 1975. *The Languages of the World*. New York: Funk and Wagnalls.

Keating, Bern. (Albert Moldvay, photo.) 1967. "Pakistan: Problems of a Two-part Land." *National Geographic* 131.1 (Jan.).

Kenney, Nathaniel T. (James P. Blair, photo.) 1965. "Ethiopian Adventure." *National Geographic* 127.4 (April).

Keyes, Nelson Beecher. 1962. *Reader's Digest Story of the Bible World*. Pleasantville, N.Y.: Reader's Digest Association.

Kennicutt, Wally. 1989. *Alphabet Roots*. Waxhaw, N.C.: Summer Institute of Linguistics.

Kham, Nguyen Khac. 1967. *An Introduction to Vietnamese Culture*. Tokyo: The Center for East Asian Cultural Studies.

Khorenats'i, Moses. 1978. *History of the Armenians*. Robert W. Thomson, trans. Cambridge, Mass.: Harvard Univ. Press.

Kilmer, Anne Draffkorn, Richard L. Crocker, and Robert R. Brown. 1976. *Sound from Silence: Recent Discoveries in Ancient Near Eastern Music*. Berkeley, Calif.: Bit Enki Pub.

King James Bible [folio page]. 1611. S.I.: s.n.

King Seijong Memorial Society. 1970. *King Seijong the Great: A Biography of Korea's Most Famous King*. Seoul, Korea: King Seijong Memorial Society.

Koestler, Arthur. 1964. *The Act of Creation*. New York: Macmillan.

Korea, Republic of [South Korea]. 1978. *A Handbook of Korea*. Seoul, Korea: Ministry of Culture and Information of the Republic of Korea.

Kotker, Norman, ed. 1969. *The Horizon History of China*. New York: American Heritage.

Kramer, Samuel Noah, and the editors of Time-Life Books. 1967. *Cradle of Civilization*. New York: Time-Life Books.

Kravitz, Nathaniel. 1972. *3000 Years of Hebrew Literature: Hebrew Literature from the Earliest Time through the 20th Century*. Chicago: Swallow Press.

"Kukai." 1986. *The New Encyclopaedia Britannica*. Micropaedia.

Kurkjian, Vahan M. 1964. *A History of Armenia*. New York: Armenian General Benevolent Union of America.

Lahiff, B., and Alexandre de Rhodes. 1967. *New Catholic Encyclopedia*. Washington, D.C.: Catholic Univ. of America.

Lancashire, D. 1958. "Chinese Language Reform." *The Bible Translator* 9.1 (Jan.).

Landis, Beth. 1969. *Exploring Music: The Senior Book*. New York: Holt, Rinehart & Wilson.

Last, Geoffrey, and Richard Pankhurst. (Eric Robson, illus.) 1969. *A History of Ethiopia in Pictures*. 4th ed. Addis Ababa: Oxford Univ. Press.

Latourette, Kenneth Scott. 1937. *A History of the Expansion of Christianity*, Vol. 1, *The First Five Centuries*. New York: Harper.

Lee, Sang-Beck. 1960. *The Origin of Hangul*. Douglas Malcom, trans. National Museum of Korea, series A., vol. 3. S.l.: s.n.

Lewis, Arthur. 1904. *The Life of the Rev. E. J. Peck Among the Eskimos*. New York: A.C. Armstrong & Son.

Lewis, Bernard, ed. 1976. *Islam and the Arab World: Faith, People, Culture*. New York: Alfred A. Knopf; American Heritage.

Liang, Shih-Chiu. 1981. *A New Practical Chinese-English Dictionary*. Taipei, Taiwan: The Far East Book Co.

Library of Congress. 1968. *Papermaking: Art and Craft*. Washington, D.C.: Library of Congress.

Library of Congress Division for the Blind and Physically Handicapped. N.d. *Braille Alphabet and Numerals*. Washington, D.C.: Library of Congress.

Lings, Martin. 1978. *The Quranic Art of Calligraphy and Illumination*. Boulder, Colo.: Shambhala Pub.

Liu, Stella S.F. 1976. *Decoding and Comprehension in Reading Chinese*. Detroit, Mich.: Wayne State Univ.

Louis, Frederic. 1969. *Japan: Art and Civilization*. New York: Abrams.

Lowery, George. 1977. "Notable Persons in Cherokee History: Sequoyah or George Gist." *Journal of Cherokee Studies* (Fall).

Lukoff, Fred. 1974. "Korean Language." *The New Encyclopaedia Britannica*. Macropaedia 10.

Lutheran Church (Missouri Synod Deaf Ministry.) N.d. *Eyes That Hear*. St. Louis, Mo.: Lutheran Church, Missouri Synod.

MacFarquhar, Roderick. 1981. "The Forbidden City." *Newsweek*.

MacLeish, Kenneth. (Dean Conger, photo.) 1966. "Abraham: A Friend of God." *National Geographic* 130.6 (Dec.).

Marcus, Joyce. 1980. "Zapotec Writing." *Scientific American* 242.2 (Feb.).

Marcus, Joyce. 1983. "The Style of the Huamelupan Stone Monuments." In *The Cloud People: Divergent Evolution of the Zapotec and Mixtec Civilization*. Kent V. Flannery and Joyce Marcus, eds. New York: Academic Press.

Marr, David G. 1981. *Vietnamese Tradition on Trial, 1920-1945*. Berkeley, Los Angeles: Univ. of Calif. Press.

Marsh, Donald B. 1947. "Canada's Caribou Eskimos." *National Geographic* 95.1 (Jan.).

Martin, Samuel E. 1972. "Nonalphabetic Writing Systems: Some Observations." In *Language by Ear and by Eye: The Relationships Between Speech and Reading*. James F. Kavanagh, ed. Cambridge, Mass.: MIT Press.

Matthews, Samuel W. (Winfred Parks, photo., Robert C. Magis, artist.) 1974. "The Phoenicians: Sea Lords of Antiquity." *National Geographic* 146.2 (Aug.).

"Mayan Calendar." 1986. *The New Encyclopaedia Britannica*. Micropaedia.

Mazzarino, Santo. 1966. *The End of the Ancient World*. George Holmes, trans. New York: Alfred A. Knopf.

McDowell, Bart. (James P. Blair, photo.) 1970. "Orissa: Past and Promise in an Indian State." *National Geographic* 138.4 (Oct.).

McEvedy, Colin. 1967. *The Penguin Atlas of Ancient History*. England: Penguin Books.

McIntyre, Loren. 1973. "The Lost Empire of the Incas." *National Geographic* 144.6 (Dec.).

McLean, John. 1890. *James Evans: Inventor of the Syllabic System of the Cree Language*. Toronto: Methodist Mission Rooms.

McMurtrie, Douglas C. [1938] 1943. *The Book: The Story of Printing and Bookmaking*. [New York: Covici Friede.] London: Oxford Univ. Press.

Menninger, Karl. 1969. *Number Words and Number Symbols: A Cultural Heritage of Numbers*. Cambridge, Mass.: MIT Press.

Metropolitan Museum of Art. 1975. *From the Land of the Scythians: Ancient Treasures from the Museums of the U.S.S.R., 3000 B.C.-100 B.C.* New York: New York Graphic Society.

Michaud, Roland, and Sabrina Michaud. 1973. "Bold Horseman of the Steppes." *National Geographic* 144.5 (Nov.).

Miller, Harry. (Naresh Bedi and Rajesh Bedi, photos.) 1970. "The Cobra: India's Good Snake." *National Geographic* 138.3 (Sept.).

The Modern Vai Syllabary. N.d. Unpublished.

Morgan, James K. 1973. "Last Stand for the Bighorn." *National Geographic* 144.3 (Sept.).

Morley, Sylvanus Griswold. 1975. *An Introduction to the Study of the Maya Hieroglyphs*. New York: Dover Pub.

Morris, Joe Alex. (John Schofield, photo.) 1961. "Venice: Twilighted Splendor Floats Serene Amid a Tide of Change." *National Geographic* 119.4 (April).

Museum of the Alphabet Staff. N.d. *Derivation of Cyrillic and Roman Alphabets: Answer Key*. Unpublished.

Museum Pieces. N.d. Black Stone Tablet of Shulgi [tablet]. New York: Museum Pieces.

Music for the Blind and Physically Handicapped. S.l.: s.n.

Nakanishi, Akira. 1980. *Writing Systems of the World: Alphabets, Syllabaries, Pictograms*. Tokyo, Japan; Rutland, Ver.: Charles E. Tuttle.

National Association of the Deaf. 1970. *A Basic Course in Manual Communication*. Silver Spring., Md.: National Association of the Deaf.

National Geographic Society. 1978. Sticks and shells chart in "Seaways to Distant Islands" [advertisement]. *National Geographic* 153.5 (May).

National Geographic Society. 1974. *The World of the American Indian*. Washington, D.C.: National Geographic Soc.

National Geographic Society. 1976. "Peoples of the Soviet Union" [map]. *National Geographic* 149.2 (Feb.).

National Geographic Society. 1978. "Middle East" [map]. *National Geographic* 154.3 (Sept.).

National Geographic Society. 1980. "Peoples of China" [map]. David Jeffrey, text auth. *National Geographic* 158.1 (July).

Newnham, Richard, and Tan Lin-Tung. 1971. *About Chinese*. Harmondsworth, Eng.: Penguin Books.

Nguyen, Dinh-Hoa. N.d. *Alexandre De Rhodes' Dictionary* (1651). Carbondale: Southern Ill. Univ.

Nixon, Richard M. (B. Anthony Stewart, photo.) 1959. "Russia as I Saw it." *National Geographic* 116.6 (Dec.).

Ober, J. Hambleton. 1965. *Writing: Man's Greatest Invention*. New York: Astor-Honor.

Ogg, Oscar. 1961. *The 26 Letters*. New York: Thomas Crowell.

Packer, James I., Merrill C. Tenney, and William White, eds. 1980. *The Bible Almanac*. Nashville: Thomas Nelson.

Panini. 1891? *Ashtadhyayi*. Srisa Chandra Vasu, trans. Delhi: Motilal Banarsidass; Ministry of Education.

Panini. 1987. *Ashtadhyayi*. Sumitra Mangesh Katre, trans. Austin: Univ. of Texas Press.

Pearlman, Moshe. 1973. *In the Footsteps of Moses*. Israel: NATEEV.

Pedersen, Holger. 1959. *The Discovery of Language*. John Webster Spargo, trans. Bloomington: Indiana Univ. Press.

Pei, Mario. 1961. *Talking Your Way Around the World*. New York: Harper & Row.

Peterson, Frederick A. 1961. *Ancient Mexico*. New York: G.P. Putnam's Sons.

Pfeiffer, Robert Henry. 1947. *Ancient Alphabets*. Cambridge, Mass.: Semitic Museum, Harvard Univ.

Pierpont Morgan Library. N.d. *Pages from the Past*. New York: Pierpont Morgan Library.

Pincerle, Marc. 1959. *An Illustrated History of Music*. New York: Reynal.

Pittman, Dean. 1948. *Practical Linguistics*. S.l.: s.n.

Pittman, Richard S. N.d. *An Ill Wind?* Unpublished.

Pittman, Richard S. N.d. *Armenian Alphabet*. Unpublished.

Pittman, Richard S. N.d. *Panini, the Insightful, Industrious Researcher*. Unpublished.

Porter, C. Foyne. 1964. "The Miracle of the Talking Leaves." In *Our Indian Heritage*. Philadelphia: Chilton.

Provencher, Ronald. 1975. *Mainland Southeast Asia: An Anthropological Perspective*. Pacific Palisades, Calif.: Goodyear Pub.

Putman, John J. (Stanley Breeden, Rajesh Bedi, Belinda Wright, photos.) 1976. "India Struggles to Save Her Wildlife." *National Geographic* 150.3 (Sept.).

Pyles, Thomas. 1971. *The Origins and Development of the English Language*. New York: Harcourt Brace Jovanovich.

R. H. Lowie Museum of Anthropology. *The Chronicle of the Kiowa Indians (1832-1892)*. Berkeley: Univ. of California.

Rabin, Chaim. 1973. *A Short History of the Hebrew Language*. Jerusalem: Jewish Agency.

Reischauer, Edwin O. 1977. *The Japanese*. Cambridge, Mass.: Belknap Press of Harvard Univ. Press.

Rhodes, Alexandre de. 1651. *Dictionarium Annamiticum Lusitanum et Latinum*. Rome, Italy: Sacrae Congregationis de Propaganda Fide Missionario Apostolico.

Rodenberg, Louis W. 1955. *The Story of Embossed Books for the Blind*. New York: American Foundation for the Blind.

Ross, Allen P. 1977. *A Hebrew Handbook*. Rev. ed. Dallas: Dallas Theological Seminary.

Ruskin, Gertrude McDaris. 1970. *Sequoyah: Cherokee Indian Cadmus*. Weaverville, N.C.: Crowder's Printing.

Sampson, Geoffrey. 1985. *Writing Systems: A Linguistic Introduction*. Stanford, Calif.: Stanford Univ. Press.

Schafer, Edward H., and the editors of Time-Life Books. 1967. *Ancient China*. History of World Cultures. New York: Time-Life Books.

Schele, Linda. 1985. *Notebook for the Maya Hieroglyphic Writing Workshop at Texas*. Austin, Tex.: Univ. of Texas at Austin, Institute of Latin American Studies.

Schmandt-Besserat, Denise. 1978. "The Earliest Precursor of Writing." *Scientific American* 238.6 (June).

Schoville, Keith N. 1984. *Sign, Symbol, Script: An Exhibition on the Origins of Writing and the Alphabet*. Madison, Wis.: Univ. of Wis., Dept. of Hebrew and Semitic Studies.

Schreider, Frank, and Helen Schreider. 1960. "From the Hair of Siva." *National Geographic* 118.4 (Oct.).

Scofield, John. 1963. "India in Crisis." *National Geographic* 123.5 (May).

Scribner, Sylvia, and Michael Cole. 1981. *The Psychology of Literacy*. Cambridge, Mass.: Harvard Univ. Press.

Seidensticker, Edward. 1961. *Japan*. Life World Library. New York: Time-Life.

Setton, Kenneth M. 1962. "A New Look at Medieval Europe." *National Geographic* 122.6 (Dec.).

Severin, Tim. (Richard Greenhill, photo.) 1982. "In the Wake of Sinbad." *National Geographic* 162.1 (July).

Shaw, E. J. (Jorge Nunez, illus.) 1973. *Egypt*. Great Civilizations. Loughborough, Eng.: Ladybird Books, Ltd.

Sherrard, Philip, and the editors of Time-Life Books. 1966. *Byzantium*. New York: Time-Life Books.

Shopen, Timothy. 1979. *Languages and Their Status*. Cambridge, Mass.: Winthrop.

Sibbett, Ed, Jr. 1979. *Celtic Design Coloring Book*. New York: Dover.

Simons, Gerald, and the editors of Time-Life Books. 1970. *Barbarian Europe*. New York: Time-Life Books.

Singh, Raghubir. 1977. "The Pageant of Rajasthan." *National Geographic* 151.2 (Feb.).

Smith, Bradley. 1968. *Mexico: A History in Art*. Garden City, N.J.: Doubleday.

Smith, Mary Elizabeth. 1973. *Picture Writing from Ancient Southern Mexico: Mixtec Signs and Maps*. Norman: Univ. of Okla. Press.

Smith, Mary Elizabeth. 1983. "The Mixtec Writing System." In *The Cloud People: Divergent Evolution of the Zapotec and Mixtec Civilization*. Kent V. Flannery and Joyce Marcus, eds. New York: Academic Press.

Smith, Michael N., and Victor M. Afanasief. 1970. *Introduction to Russian*. New York: Holt, Rinehart and Winston.

Smithsonian Institution. N.d. *Chinese Calligraphy*. Freer Gallery of Art.

Soustelle, Jacques. 1979. *Los Olmecas*. S.l.: s.n.

Soustelle, Jacques. 1983. *Los Olmecas*. Juan José Utrilla, trans. Mexico: Fondo de Cultura Económica.

Southern Living. 1988 "Where an Alphabet was Born." (April).

Soviet Life. (Aug., 1974.)

Speiser, E. A. (H. M. Herget, illus.) 1951. "Ancient Mesopotamia: A Light that Did Not Fail." *National Geographic* 99.1 (Jan.).

Steel, Richard. N.d. [Comments concerning a trip to San Juan.] Unpublished.

Sten, Maria. 1978. *Codices of Mexico and their Extraordinary History*. Carolyn B. Czitrom, trans. Mexico City: CIPSA.

Stilman, Galina, Leon Stilman, and William E. Harkins. 1972. *Introductory Russian Grammar*. Lexington, Mass.: Xerox College Pub.

Stirling, Matthew W. (W. Langdon Kihn, artist.) 1949. "Nomads of the Far North." *National Geographic* 96.4 (Oct.).

Stuart, George E., ed. 1983. *Peoples and Places of the Past: The National Geographic Illustrated Cultural Atlas of the Ancient World*. Washington, D. C.: National Geographic Society.

Thompson, J. Eric S. 1956. *The Rise and Fall of Maya Civilization*. Norman, Okla.: Univ. of Okla. Press.

Thompson, J. Eric S. 1972. *The Dresden Codex*. Philadelphia: American Philosophical Society.

Thorpe, James. 1975. *The Gutenberg Bible: Landmark in Learning*. Pasadena, Calif.: Castle Press.

Tobita, Shigeo. 1971. "Levels of Style in Japanese." *The Bible Translator* 22.2 (April).

Toby, L. F. 1973. *The Art of Hebrew Lettering*. Israel: Rolf Schuster.

Toynbee, Arnold, ed. 1973. *Half the World: The History and Culture of China and Japan*. New York: Holt, Rinehart and Winston.

Tracy, Walter. 1964. "The Flourishing Reed: Arabic Scripts." In *Alphabet International Annual*. Birmingham, Great Britain: s.n.

Tracy, Walter. N.d. *Facing the East: Baseline*. London: Typographic Systems International.

Trager, George Leonard. 1974. *Writing and Writing Systems*. Current Trends in Linguistics 12. The Hague: Mouton.

Trans World Radio. 1983. "All Armenia is Listening!" (Feb.).

Trever, John C. N.d. *The Untold Story of Qumran*. Westwood, N.J.: Fleming H. Revell.

Tsien, Tsuen-Hsuin. 1962. *Written on Bamboo and Silk: The Beginnings of Chinese Books and Inscriptions*. Chicago: Univ. of Chicago Press.

Uehara, Tayoaki, and Gisaburo N. Kiyose. 1974. *Fundamentals of Japanese*. Bloomington: Indiana Univ. Press.

"Ulfilas." 1971. *Encyclopaedia Britannica* 22.

Unger, Merrill F. 1954. *Archaeology and the Old Testament*. Grand Rapids, Mich.: Zondervan.

United Bible Societies. 1972. *The Book of a Thousand Tongues*. Rev. ed. London: United Bible Societies.

Univ. Museum. N.d. Page from a Third Century Gospel of Matthew (1:14-24) found at Oxyrhyncus, Egypt [postcard]. Philadelphia: Univ. of Penn. Museum.

Vaillant, George C. 1950. *Aztecs of Mexico: Origin, Rise and Fall of the Aztec Nation*. Baltimore, Md.: Penguin Books.

Van Der Meer, E. 1959. *Atlas of the Early Christian World*. Translated and edited by Mary E. Hedlund and H. H. Rowley. London: Thomas Nelson & Sons.

Van Deuren, A. 1970. *Illustrated Dictionary of Bible Manners and Customs*. S.l.: Oliphants.

Vervliet, Hendrik D. L., ed. 1972. *The Book through 5000 Years: A Survey by Fernand Bauden and Others*. New York: Phaidon.

Wallis, Ethel. 1968. *God Speaks Navajo*. New York: Harper & Row.

Ward, Fred. 1975. "The Changing World of Canada's Crees." *National Geographic* 147.4 (April).

Ward, Fred. 1980. "In Long-forbidden Tibet." *National Geographic* 157.2 (Feb.).

Wauchope, Robert, and Gordon R. Willey, eds. 1965. *Handbook of Middle American Indians: Archaeology of Southern Mesoamerica*. Austin: Univ. of Texas Press.

Weaver, Muriel Porter. 1981. *The Aztecs, Maya and their Predecessors: Archaeology of Mesoamerica*. New York: Academic Press.

Wegener, G. S. 1963. *6000 Years of the Bible*. New York: Harper & Row.

Weinberg, Werner. 1985. *The History of Hebrew Plene Spelling*. Cincinnati: Hebrew Union College Press.

Wellard, James. 1964. *The Great Sahara*. New York: E.P. Dutton.

Wentzel, Volkmar. 1948. "Splendor Lingers in Rajputana." *National Geographic* 94.4 (Oct.).

Whitecatton, Joseph W. 1977. *The Zapotec: Princes, Priests and Peasants*. Norman, Okla.: Univ. of Okla.

Wieger, L. 1965. *Chinese Characters*. (Paragon Book.) New York: Dover.

Wilkins, Thurman. 1970. *Cherokee Tragedy*. New York: Macmillan.

Wills, Don. 1980. *Morning Calm* 3. S.l.: Church of England Korean Mission.

Wilson, Steven C., and Karen C. Hayden. 1981. "Where Oil and Wildlife Mix." *National Geographic* 159.2 (Feb.).

Wood, Roger, photo. 1975. *An Introduction to Saudi Arabian Antiquities*. Kingdom of Saudi Arabia: Ministry of Education, Dept. of Antiquities and Museums.

"World's Oldest Musical Notation Deciphered on Cuneiform Tablet." 1980. *Biblical Archaeology Review* 6.5 (Sept./Oct.).

Young, Egerton Ryerson. N.d. "James Evans as the Inventor of the Syllabic Characters." *Canadian Methodist Magazine*. (English Wesleyan Missionary Society; British & Foreign Bible Society.)

Zierer, Otto, ed. 1978. *Concise History of Great Nations: History of China*. New York: Leon Amiel.

АБВГДЕЁЖЗИЙКЛМНОП
абвгдеёжзийклмноп
a b v g d ye yo zh z i -y k l m n o p

The Cyrillic alphabet has undergone several revisions and many adaptations. In slightly different form, Cyrillic is the official alphabet for the following Slavic languages: Russian, White Russian, Ukrainian, Bulgarian, Macedonian, and Serbian, the last 2 spoken in Yugoslavia.

Cyrillic-type alphabets for Slavic languages other than Russian vary from the Russian in the following ways:

Byelorussian (White Russian)
  plus i, ў; minus и, щ, ъ

Ukrainian
  plus є, і, ї; minus ё, ъ, ы, э

Bulgarian
  minus ё, ы, э

Serbian
  plus ђ, џ, љ, њ, ћ, ј;
  minus щ, ъ, ы, ь, э, ю, я

Macedonian
  plus ѓ, ќ, ѕ, љ, њ, џ
  minus ё, й, ъ, ы, ь, э, ю, я

Polish, Czech, Sorbian, and Wendish are West Slavic languages that use the Roman alphabet.

back (hard) tongue position

A = a as in father
Э = e as in ten
Ы = i as in it
О = o as in port
У = u as in duty
Ъ = backing of consonant

turn handle
to change
tongue position

Front and Back Tongue

The Cyrillic Alphabet represent Russian language by providing the two tongue positions of sp and back.

Vowels

There are 10 vowels,
  5 pronounced with t
  5 pronounced with te
  (as written on the tongue

Compare

Fronted (soft)			
Russian	Pronunciation	Meaning	Rus
ЛЮК	l'ook⁷	"hatch"	ЛУ
ВЯЛ	v'al	"withered"	ВА
НЁС	n'os	"carried"	НО

Consonants

Two letters of the alphabet, b nounced. They indicate front a of the consonants that prece b fronts a consonant, when n occurs frequently.
ъ backs a consonant, and inst ing front vowel. It occurs infre

Compare

Fronted (soft)			
Russian	Pronunciation	Meaning	Rus
СЕСТЬ	sest⁷	"sit down"	СЪ
БРАТЬ	brat⁷	"take"	БР
УГОЛЬ	oogol⁷	"coal"	УГ

the raised '⁷' indicates fronti